**Racial
Discrimination
and Public Policy
in the
United States**

This book is published for the Center on International Race Relations in their *Race and Nations Series.* The Center seeks the wider recognition of the role of race in international affairs, and through its research and teaching programs develops a systematic analysis of race in American foreign relations.

Racial Discrimination and Public Policy in the United States

Richard M. Burkey
University of Denver

Heath Lexington Books
D.C. Heath and Company
Lexington, Massachusetts
Toronto   London

Table of Contents

List of Tables

Foreword

Law is for the most part an instrument of the strong, a reflection of the desires, the values, and interests of the strong. As Rousseau has pointed out, even the spirit of law usually favors the strong against the weak and the man who has against the man who has not. The often-seen courthouse inscription "rule of law and not of men" is merely an expression of an unreachable ideal, for even under a rule of law, law is made by men and administered by men. Moreover, in all instances of law, whether the strong is defined in terms of a constitutional consensus, winners of an election, victors in a civil war or tyrannical dictatorship, force is the ultimate sanction of law. Without the sanction of force, law is often merely legal fiction.

Public policy, therefore, be it to enforce racial discrimination or to combat racial discrimination, is subject to the same categories of societal forces to which all laws are subject. Among those categories are racist values and racial discrimination themselves. And given the systemic nature of racism and racial discrimination, a society that is attempting to effect public policy to combat racial discrimination may ultimately be attempting the impossible.

As a phenomenon especially peculiar to racially fragmented Euro-American societies, racial discrimination is a many-sided problem which defies ultimate solution except through a multi-faceted and comprehensive application of a multi-faceted and comprehensive remedy. The complex nature of racial discrimination, derived as it is from the convergence of often little understood psycho-cultural factors and social power, makes the task of eliminating it through any means difficult enough in itself. The task of public policy to combat racial discrimination, however, is made even more arduous by the fact that many of the assumptions inherent in and the continuing traditions supportive of racially discriminatory practices place the primary responsibility for combating these practices on the perpetrators of racial discrimination. That is, public policy imposes on the discriminator the responsibility to act against what he has long perceived to be right and in his own interest. On the other hand, traditions of racial discrimination tend to minimize the victim's participatory responsibility in combating the problem. In other words, the assumptions underlying traditions of racial discrimination dictate that those most sensitive to its workings and effects be allowed least participation in the formation and implementation of policy to combat discrimination, while those least sensitive to and whose values and interests have been maximized by racial discrimination have primary and ultimate responsibility for making and enforcing the policy.

Furthermore, because of the nature of racial discrimination, public policy to

Before Reality

eliminate or ameliorate it is usually most reflective of the discriminator's racist assumptions and interests and least reflective of the discriminatee's values and interests. In that regard, one may seriously question whether a society such as that of the United States is really capable of legislating and enforcing effective public policy to combat racial discrimination. It would appear that the most effective function of such legislation is simply that of providing an aura of legitimacy for more direct political action to combat racial discrimination—particularly political action by the victims of racial discrimination.

What follows is an attempt to clarify the above statements and to analyze their implications both for policy research and policy-making in the area of racial discrimination. As stated earlier, racial discrimination is the result of the convergence of psycho-cultural factors and social power which leads to the quantitative and qualitative exclusion or restriction of a group from equal participation in a society's reward system. The excluded or restricted group is socially defined *a priori* in terms of some biologically inherited physical characteristic which acts as a signaling device in the mind of the discriminator. The signal resulting from the discriminator's perception of the physical characteristic identifies its bearer as a member of the group to be excluded or restricted. The rationale for exclusion derives from pejorative assumptions and characteristics ascribed to all individuals bearing that same distinctive physical characteristic—that is, from racism.

Racism—the ascription of assumed superior/inferior status to members of physically identifiable groups solely on the basis of their biologically inherited physical differences—is not by itself a sufficient cause of racial discrimination. It may lead to attitudes of dislike and distrust but not necessarily to racially exclusive behavior reflective of those attitudes. It may lead to feelings of hostility and antipathy for members of another racial group, but even this by itself is insufficient to bring about racial discrimination. If the racist is to translate his racial biases and prejudices into racial discrimination, his racial group must be politically and economically dominant. (A Frenchman in independent Guinee may still consider Sekou Touré "un sauvage noir" but he dare not act as his pre-1958 compatriot did.) In racist Mississippi, for example, where black economic boycotts have driven some white racists into poverty, there are still white racist businessmen who dare not discriminate against blacks for fear of a like fate. Hence, racial discrimination is a function of the convergence of racism and power—the power to translate racism into racially discriminatory behavior. Any policies to combat racial discrimination must be aimed, therefore, at eliminating or neutralizing the *ability* of the racist to resort to acts of racial discrimination, or minimally at making the cost of exercising that ability prohibitive.

It is further in the nature of racial discrimination to be self-serving. It engenders and fixes the conditions that provide concrete justification for racist assumptions. In a functional sense, racial discrimination is the process whereby the dominating racist attempts to concretize his concept of his victim's inferiority. Successful racial discrimination thus leads its victim eventually to conform in reality to the preconceived reified notion of what he is in the mind of the discriminator—a *thing* whose worth is determined only by how it serves the interests of the discriminator. Accordingly, in the system of United States slavery, an African slave was only chattel until accorded the nondistinction of being three-fifths a person (a human being) when this suited the interests of his masters. Even when the African in the United States was finally accorded the legal status of citizenship the Americanization process was designed to keep him at best a second-class human being who could qualify only for separate and unequal treatment.

It is hardly coincidental that in both Europe and the United States the ending of the slave trade and the physical liberation of the slaves was quickly followed by so many pseudo-scientific theories about the lower form of human nature possessed by the black man. Colonialism and Jim Crowism attempted to demonstrate the reality underlying the white man's assumption of the black man's inferior status among the children of God. Once the black *thing* was accorded at least humanity, it had to be kept as nearly non-human as possible. The ability to make real the notion of the victim of racial discrimination as an inferior human being set the stage for total discrimination. Thus, being born black in the United States has meant nonqualification for quality education, which in turn has meant nonqualification for good jobs, to earn less income, to suffer the lowest standard of living, etc., back to the reality of being black in an anti-black society.

Another aspect of racial discrimination—perhaps the most difficult to deal with in matters of public policy—is the institutionalization of racial discrimination. Given the multiplier effect of racial discrimination, it is quite easy for discrimination to become institutionalized throughout a society. Once institutionalization occurs, it becomes part of the socialization process which conditions and more or less fixes attitudes and behavior in the relations between the discriminator and the victim of discrimination. Race relations then become a matter of accepted and often unconscious role-playing in which the discriminator is expected to and in fact plays the superior role, and the victim of discrimination expects to, and in fact does, play the inferior part.

That which under noninstitutionalized racist conditions would be considered a manifestation of overt and blatant racism is viewed simply as a matter of politics or economics or anything other than racial discrimination. Thus, the Vice President of the United States in 1970 could proclaim publicly that the exclusion of blacks from major American universities was simply a matter of blacks not being qualified. Or a black-skinned minister at the funeral of one of several black youths murdered by legal guns in Augusta, Georgia, could claim the death of those black youths was simply the result of their having disobeyed their parents by participating in Augusta racial demonstrations. Or a California psychologist can claim that blacks perform as a group less successfully on intelligence tests because they are inherently (through heredity) less intelligent than whites. Or a Washington, D.C. sociologist can claim that blacks perform best only after having been exposed to white peer group influences. Or the contention can be made that poor blacks are poor because they are lazy and are not inclined to hard work. That is, the victim of discrimination is blamed (often believing the accusation) for the condition imposed upon him by the discriminator.

After more than three centuries of systematic attempts to exclude the African-American from the affairs of men in the United States—after more than three centuries of an un-think process vis-a-vis the Black man—black and white alike have difficulty seeing racism at the bottom of the black/white conflict in the United States. Accordingly, any attempts to challenge the old relationships between black and white are often met with hostility by both blacks and whites. It is only after a resocialization process has begun to take effect that the old relationships can be effectively challenged. Such was the case with the United States Supreme Court's decision striking down the separate but equal doctrine which led to the movement for integration. Such was the case with the 1966 Black Power Movement which heightened the power struggle between blacks and whites.

Many blacks and whites opposed the 1954 decision until its resocialization effect had legitimized attempts to desegregate schools and integration became the vogue. Blacks and whites opposed (and many still oppose) the 1966 Black Power Movement until its resocialization effect had begun to legitimize the concept of racial pluralism. The latter is particularly hard to accept by many whites and blacks because unlike the assimilationist Civil Rights Movement of the 1950s and early 1960s it comes to grips with the seemingly irreconcilable inflexibility of institutionalized racial discrimination and the irreducibility of race. It is difficult particularly for the liberal white and psychologically assimilated black-skinned American to accept because it dismisses as irrelevant any policies or programs that do not aim specifically to change the servant/master relationship between black and white. It disturbs this latter group because it reduces black/white relations to what they really are presently—institutionalized superior white racist power vs. institutionalized black weakness.

It is this fact—the persistence of institutionalized racial discrimination and the irreducibility of race—that brings us to the last part of the opening statement regarding the enduring efficacy of public policy to combat racial discrimination.

The irreducibility of race is obvious. Afro-Americans and Euro-Americans are not appreciably different from their original African and European racial stocks. For all practical purposes, race in a biological sense is irreducible. And where racial discrimination has been institutionalized, race in the social sense is equally as irreducible. Of the two, however, only race in the social sense offers any probable chance of being eliminated within an acceptable time span. This, of course, calls for radical institutional change in a racist society. It is the crux of the questions posed for the formulation of public policy to combat racial discrimination.

Can a racist society legislate public policy to bring about radical institutional changes necessary to eliminate racial discrimination? Can *public policy* in a racist (anti-black) society effect the kind of radical institutional changes necessary for changing the servant/master relationship between black and white to one of equality? What is the *probability* that a racist (anti-black) society *will* legislate and enforce public policy to achieve the radical institutional changes necessary for changing the servant/master relationship between black and white to one of equality?

The first two questions are theoretical and their answers are implicit in the third question. Despite the antithetical relationship between racism and combating racial discrimination, one can conceive (one must conceive) of a racist taking unpleasant measures, limited though they may be, to circumvent or neutralize his own ability to translate his racism into racially discriminatory behavior. Man is not incapable of curbing his activities while still adhering to the values that ordinarily inform those activities. Whether a society in which racism has been internalized and racial discrimination institutionalized to the point of being essential and inherently functioning components of that society—a culture in which racial discrimination has, from its inception, been a regulative force for maintaining stability and growth and for maximizing other cultural values— whether such a society *of itself* can even legislate (let alone enforce) public policy to effectively combat racial discrimination is most doubtful. The history of man offers no evidence of any society consciously legislating itself out of existence. To the contrary, when a society has adhered stubbornly to dysfunctional values and their institutional representations, radical cultural changes have occurred only after the demise of that society. And the demise has either been a slow death brought on by internal societal forces pressuring the dominant cultural unit or it has been a quick death effected by some extra-societal force.

Put another way, questions one and two are: Can the present variety of Euro-American (i.e. white—the only culture traditionally referred to in racial terms by its bearers) culture found in United States society, intimately bound up in and partly a product of white racism, be expanded to include black as a value?

Put in the popular language of today: In American society, can black really become beautiful in itself? Again, theoretically, it is possible. Cultures must expand or become stagnant and eventually die, destroying the societies supporting them.

U.S. culture not only has demonstrated its capacity to expand and incorporate "foreign" values, but from its inception pluralism has been one of its overriding informing values. It has been more or less able to reconcile contrary (if not contradictory) values such as human rights vs. property rights, state rights vs. church rights, local government vs. national government, individual rights vs. the common good, private ownership vs. corporate and public ownership, labor vs. management, etc. Historically each of these adjustments was accompanied with deeply felt aberrations and dislocations in U.S. society and led to the dissolution of established institutions and the creation of new ones. Moreover, each adjustment also led to the release of new cultural energies that increased the potency of the expanded dominant cultural unit.

In terms of race, however, each of these adjustments was made not only without incorporating the black American into the expanded cultural unit, but more often than not at the expense of the black American whose role was often that of subsidizing the expansion. The beginning of a free white society through the elimination of white indentured servitude in the latter part of the 17th century was a function of the enslavement of the African. Economic growth and development of the young United States through the wedding of the industrializing North to the agricultural South was largely born by the manpower of the enslaved black. After the subcultures of the North and South clashed in the Civil War, Jim Crowism brought the two sections back together.

The last great domestic crisis—the threatening class struggle consequent to post-Civil War industrialization—was again resolved without regard for the black. In fact, one party to the struggle—white labor—has become one of the greatest obstacles to the achievement of black equality. But the pursuit of the better life for the worker in the United States, like the pronouncements of the Founding Fathers on the inalienable rights, was never meant to include the *black thing*. And again through his imposed poverty and unemployment the black man subsidized the entrance of another group of white men into the dominant cultural unit from which he himself was excluded.

Today's crises over war and peace, between young and old, between establishment and anti-establishment have yet to be reconciled. These crises revolve around issues that reflect differences in basic values and interests. The black/white issue and white racism are intimately tied to the conflict. On the surface it appears that the crises cannot be resolved without finally resolving the servant/master relationship between black and white. But when one remembers especially the Civil War and Reconstruction and the ability of United States

NEUTRALIZE

society to reconstitute itself at the expense of the black man or with no regard for his values and interests, one cannot but wonder.

The wonder is reinforced in light of the increasing disengagement of the white liberal and radical from the cause of black equality when that cause has been put in the context of black vs. white. It does not matter that black vs. white means black human and civil rights vs. white racism. White racism becomes in effect a higher good than black human and civil rights. White property rights become more important than black human rights. And we are back again where we started with chattel slavery: Blacks are reduced to "thingness" whose value is calculated against the value of white property. So there is no national outcry or mourning when black students are killed at Texas Southern University, at South Carolina State University or when black radicals like the Panthers are assassinated systematically. Fortunately for the two murdered black students at Jackson State College, their deaths came in the wake of the killing of four white students at Kent State University, and the former shared in the mourning for the latter. The white liberal and radical (from whom the impetus for racial change in the white community must come) has a black attention span proportionate only to the black's willingness to be led by whites to white defined goals.

Indeed one can wonder whether white U.S. society can legislate and enforce effective public policy to combat racial discrimination. Already white domestic energies are being successfully diverted from the issue of race and related issues by the prevailing issue of environmental pollution. Interestingly, there is little mention of or demonstrated concern for the imposed environmental and moral pollution that blacks have had to contend with in the inner cities of the country. So white eco-brigades march to clean parks and rivers, etc., that blacks cannot afford or are not allowed to use.

The above leads one to conclude that cultural expansion (the inclusion of groups outside of the dominant cultural unit) occurs only when the dominant bearers perceive the culture to be severely threatened with destruction. A racist culture, then, can move to eradicate or make racism ineffective only when racism itself becomes a serious threat to the culture and its bearers. United States society, therefore, can legislate and enforce public policy to combat racial discrimination effectively only when continued racial discrimination begins to be more a serious threat to the existing Euro-American culture than the useful regulator it has been. This assumes, of course, that the bearers of the culture are willing to perceive, and are capable of perceiving, the threat of racial discrimination to themselves. Where racial discrimination has seemingly diminished, it has been largely the result of direct political and/or economic activity of black people themselves. In fact, what public policies have been established have themselves come only after extreme political activity on the part of blacks.

Given the unique role of racism and the racial discrimination it has spawned in U.S. society, the probability of the United States establishing and enforcing effective public policy to combat racial discrimination will be to a large degree a direct function of the activities of black Americans as they make racial discrimination a riskier and costlier business for the discriminator.

In light of the above, the importance of Professor Burkey's study of the effectiveness of public policy to combat racial discrimination lies as much in the questions it raises as in those it answers. Despite the tragic history of black/white relations in the U.S., this book demonstrates that there have been changes *toward* parity in those relationships. Moreover, public policy has played a role in those changes. The changes toward parity, however, have been only slight except in black voting registration which over a period of 28 years (1940-1968) increased from 4 percent to 60.8 percent of all eligible black voters. The general picture of black/white stratification, however, has remained relatively unchanged since slavery. What this clearly means is that while the *stratified condition* of the Black American has changed per se, the pattern of black/white stratification remains relatively constant. To be black in the U.S. means to be on the bottom.

Of special significance to the policy-maker, the policy researcher and the social engineer should be Professor Burkey's identification of the factors that affect the degree of *effectiveness* (or lack thereof) of public policies directed against racial discrimination. It is only when the mechanism of a certain public policy is known that the policy can begin to be *used* intelligently to effect desired goals or discarded as dysfunctional. Without this kind of understanding, a certain public policy could ultimately be self-defeating. In terms of the credibility of public policy as a nonviolent approach to the resolution of racial conflict, a self-defeating policy or one that is perceived to be self-defeating could result in greater conflict. The credibility of public policy becomes especially critical as black Americans become increasingly aware of the persistence of seemingly unchangeable racial stratification patterns.

The study is also significant in that it identifies areas for further research and analysis. Some of Burkey's proposed research questions relate to the policy-making process itself and suggest inquiries into the role of race in that process. These questions are fundamental and answers to them are needed if the basic question of this foreword is to be answered: How can a racist society legislate and enforce effectively public policy to combat racial discrimination? Needless to say, the implications are tremendous not only for domestic public policy, but for U.S. foreign policy as well.

The United States is fast approaching its 200th birthday. It was founded on the principles of human equality and equal opportunity for all. Judged by the record of its application of those principles to black/white race relations, the United States has yet to be born. Professor Burkey's study is a large step in that direction.

Tilden J. LeMelle
Center on International Race
  Relations
University of Denver

Introduction

On December 19, 1966, the General Assembly of the United Nations adopted a resolution dealing with racial discrimination and public policy sponsored by the United Nations Institute for Training and Research (UNITAR). The title of this resolution was: "Guidelines for a Study of the Effectiveness of Policies and Measures Against Racial Discrimination" (see Appendix A). This study was to be done in several nations, and the Institute of Race Relations at the University of Denver, under the directorship of Dr. George W. Shepherd, Jr., was assigned by UNITAR the task of research in the United States.

The objectives of the UNITAR study are: (1) describe the "main traits and trends; historical background and analysis of the origins and orientations of the patterns of values, assumptions and goals connected with the prevailing racial policies;" (2) develop an "objective characterization of the situation at the end of World War II" in terms of the "structural characteristics of the multiracial society: demographic data; positions of the groups in the stratification system;" (3) analyze "the factors and trends that, up to the present, have acted to change that situation" with particular attention to "the identification and evaluation of the role played by the deliberate application of policies and measures to combat racial discrimination, compared to other influential factors;" (4) ". . . extract from the analysis and comparison, possible guidelines for better performance in the future."

As is readily apparent, these objectives will necessitate a monumental undertaking involving conceptualization, theory and research. What is necessary is (1) a preliminary effort at conceptualization and clarification of the major variables; (2) a review of the literature; and (3) an effort to ascertain some of the problems and areas that will need further research before the project can be finalized. The purposes of this book are therefore rather limited, and are to be taken as *preliminary* or exploratory: (1) to develop a theoretical perspective on the nature of discrimination and *racial* discrimination in particular; (2) to clarify the relationship of racial discrimination to such other concepts as racism, prejudice, segregation, and racial stratification; (3) to summarize the patterns of racial discrimination against Black-Americans[a] from 1619 to World War II utilizing the previously developed theoretical perspective; (4) to attempt to ascertain the extent of change in the patterns of racial discrimination and racial inequality between World War II and the present; (5) to attempt to ascertain

---

[a]This preliminary study is limited to Black-Americans for a number of tactical reasons—the availability of data on blacks, the relative lack of data on Chicanos or Spanish-Americans (this in itself illustrates the need of research), the unique status of Indian-Americans and Indian policies, and the lack of antidiscrimination policies related to the highly acculturated Chinese and Japanese-Americans (other than general civil rights for all Americans).

what social factors that, in addition to public policies, have produced these changes, if any; (6) to identify what factors or variables affect the degree of *effectiveness* of public policies directed against racial discrimination; and, (7) to itemize areas and problems for further research.

One major goal of the UNITAR study—to compare, weigh, and separate the relative influences of the various social factors, including public policy, on patterns of racial discrimination and racial inequality—is not discussed.

**Racial
Discrimination
and Public Policy
in the
United States**

1

Discrimination and Racial Relations: A Theoretical Perspective

The Nature of Discrimination

The dependent variable of the UNITAR study is racial discrimination.[a] It is this variable that is to be changed by public policy. Before any study such as the one proposed by the UNITAR guidelines can be done, this concept needs considerable clarification and analysis. One meaning of the word discrimination includes the idea of being "selective"—selective in terms of one's friends, one's tastes, one's membership in organizations, etc. This meaning is not, however, the one that is primarily used in the social science literature. Generally, most social scientists define discrimination as "unequal and disadvantageous treatment of one category of human beings by another." Vander Zanden defines discrimination as, ". . . overt action in which members of a group are accorded unfavorable treatment on the basis of their religious, ethnic or racial membership."[1] Michael Banton defines discrimination as ". . . the differential treatment of persons ascribed to particular social categories. . . ."[2] In both of these definitions, the idea of "treatment" is not spelled out. A European publication defines discrimination as ". . . any distinction, exclusion or preference made on the basis of race, colour, sex, religion, political opinion, national extraction or social origin, which has the effect of nullifying or impairing equality of opportunity or treatment in employment or occupation."[3] This definition is somewhat more explicit about the nature of the "treatment" in that it specifies "nullifying or impairing equality of opportunity," but limits discrimination to the areas of occupational and employment opportunity. Each one of these definitions is, simultaneously, too broad and too specific. Differential treatment could, theoretically, include genocide practices of Nazis against Jews, war between two national groups, as well as exclusion from one's country club. On the other hand, limiting discrimination to just races, religions, ethnic groups or the area of occupational opportunity is far too narrow a perspective since discrimination against such categories of people as students, women, aliens, classes, estates, children, etc. are not included in these definitions.

It is proposed here that discrimination (generally) be defined as: differential

---

[a]Although this generally is emphasized in the UNITAR guidelines, in the first section, it seems to be implied that "patterns of race relations" is the dependent variable (see Appendix A).

1

treatment by members of a dominant social category which functions to deny or restrict the choices of members of a subordinate social category. A brief definition would be—categorically restrictive treatment. The major elements of this definition—category, dominant and subordinate, treatment, and choice restriction—need to be further elaborated and explained.

Human beings primarily relate to other human beings on the basis of the meanings that they have regarding symbolic categories. Symbolic categories of human beings would be such words as woman, man, child, policeman, teacher, old man, hood, criminal, mentally ill, student, serf, noble, Negro, Jew, Anglo, Chicano, Southerner, American, German, wife, judge, king, etc. Single individuals are members of many such symbolic categories and behavior toward an individual will often depend upon the situational relevancy of particular categories; however, some categories in particular societies or in particular communities have categorical primacy. That is, some categories have overriding significance in any social situation. Dwarfs are dwarfs first, regardless of what else they may be—educated, old, young, male, female, student or teacher, etc. Besides this extreme example, ethnic or racial categories have or had primacy as well as "woman" in most societies.

Particular symbolic categories or statuses (or positions) often relate to other particular statuses on the basis of a power differential. One status has more power than the other, power being defined as the ability (based upon resources) to apply negative sanctions which affects behavior. These differences in social power create *dominant* and *subordinate* statuses. Examples of such relationships are teacher-student, male-female, noble-serf, warden-prisoner, white-black, Anglo-Chicano, employer-employee, old-young, German-French, etc. It is this difference in social power that enables members of the dominant category to discriminate against members of the subordinate category; discrimination cannot exist without this power differential.[b]

Discriminatory *treatment* imposed on subordinate statuses by dominant statuses can be divided into three major elements—norms, techniques, and sanctions. Discrimination in the rhetoric of contemporary liberals and radicals generally has an overt or a covert value-judgment connotation. Discrimination, by definition, is "bad," or it is a "social problem." People who discriminate are defined as "pathological" or, at best, "deviant." But, generally in the history of social systems, discrimination has been normative and institutionalized.[c] Formal and informal norms exist within a social system (a society, region, community, organization, group, etc.) that are positively sanctioned when obeyed and

[b]This implies that discriminatory practices can only be changed by changing this power difference either by a reversal of power or by the development of a balanced power situation.

[c]Recent writers give the impression that "institutional racism" is a new phenomena.

negatively sanctioned when violated. These norms are intended to restrict the choices of less powerful statuses. Formal norms appear as laws or as official policies and rules of social organizations, while informal norms appear as unwritten customary behaviors. An example of a formal discriminatory norm in the area of racial discrimination would be—Japanese cannot own any land and can only lease a particular section of land for a period not to exceed three years (The Alien Land-Holding Act passed in California in 1913). An example of an informal racially discriminatory norm would be the customary expectations about what constitutes "Negro jobs"—the low status jobs in an organization or community that are reserved for black workers.

In stable systems of human relationships, these proscribed and prescribed expectations of behavior (norms) are rarely challenged by members of the subordinant category and are considered to be part of the moral order of society by most of the members of society, including the discriminated. Women, children, students, blacks, and labor, for example, have all at one time accepted, and many have internalized, their unequal social position. Individuals in subordinant social categories within stable systems rarely challenge discriminatory norms because of fear of reprisal, fear of being rebuffed, because of apathy produced by previous failures, because of negative sanctions imposed on them by members of their *own* category, or because they believe it is wrong to do so. In such stable systems, when the norms are occasionally challenged, righteous moral indignation develops among individuals within the dominant sectors of society (and sometimes within the subordinate category; for example, the majority of women for a long period of time in the United States were indignant and disturbed by other women demanding the right to vote). It is the *challenge* to the norm, not the norm itself, that is defined as problematic (witness the outcry of many faculty members over the audacity of students demanding the right to participate in the decisions of what they have to learn).

This relative lack of challenges to discriminatory norms on the part of the discriminated raises an interesting problem. Discrimination has been distinguished from prejudice by many authors who define discrimination as behavior, and prejudice as attitudinal. But, postulating an ideal state of discrimination where none of the discriminated members challenges or violates the norms, wherein lies the behavior? Is the behavior the actions of the subordinant group dutifully keeping their place? Even when there are some challenges and violations (and this certainly always exists to some degree), is an empirical study of the extent of discrimination only to focus on the occasional behavioral acts of dominant member sanctioning (e.g., throwing a black out of a restaurant)? Such an approach would hardly ascertain the full extent of the discrimination. A more realistic empirical approach would be to first ascertain if discriminatory norms exist and then to ascertain the extent of violation and challenges. Some measure of the *effectiveness* of discrimination could be developed whereby the less the violations of the norm, the more effective the discrimination, and the greater the number of violations and dominant group reactions, the less effective the discrimination. A very relevant study that relates to this concept of effectiveness was done by Mathews and Prothro dealing with voting registration by Southern blacks. They suggest that "...race violence nowadays must be extremely massive indeed in order to have a depressing effect on Negro voting registration. Save in the most violent one or two percent of southern counties, racial violence seems to be more an indication of white weakness than of strength. Far lower rates of Negro registration are found in counties with little if any racial violence. Here Negro subordination may be so total that violence is not required to keep the Negro 'in his place' and outside of the polling booths."[4]

It is only when once-stable social systems are undergoing change that the norms which were once considered part of the moral order gradually become to be defined as social problems, along with the increasing incidents of negative sanctioning behavior. These changes are primarily due to the demands for greater freedom by a subordinant category of human beings. As this change takes place, the increasing challenges and violations at first are defined as problems and are included in social problem texts. Then gradually, and not necessarily, the discrimination itself becomes to be defined as the social problem. When this transition has occurred, the minority of individuals and groups that still continue to discriminate or attempt to discriminate are considered deviant (fascists, pathological, chauvinists, sexists, racists, reactionaries, etc.). It should be added, however, that deviant discrimination is complicated by the variety of subsystems within complex societies. What may be considered deviant by, say, the federal government, may not be considered deviant by a county in Mississippi, but "preserving our lawful heritage."

Social conflict[d] can be related to the concept of discrimination as normative. Conflict instigated primarily by a dominant group develops as discriminatory norms are imposed upon a category, as, for example, the large increases in the lynching of blacks in the period 1890-1900 as "Jim-Crow" segregation or apartheid was being established.[5] In addition, dominant-instigated conflict occurs in the form of official sanctions (legitimate violence) when institutionalized norms have been violated, as in the crushing of the Nat Turner rebellion. Conflict caused by a subordinant category develops when members of this status challenge the system of institutionalized discriminatory norms, such as in the labor strikes of the nineteenth and early twentieth centuries, or in the student protests and black movements of today.

The first major aspect of the concept of "differential treatment," then, is

---

[d]The attempt to eliminate, injure, neutralize, or dominate one's rivals over common goals by violent or nonviolent means.

norms. The second element of what is meant by treatment involves *techniques*. Discriminatory techniques are those methods that are utilized to implement the discriminatory norms. Techniques may be overt or covert. An example of the obvious or covert form of discrimination would be an advertisement in the employment section of a newspaper stating that no Orientals need apply (the norm in this case is—Orientals are not to be hired in this occupation). Other examples would be the posting of signs saying "Mexicans and dogs stay out," or "For men only," or "All niggers are to be out of town by sunset." Even the giving of keys to the more elegant lavatories of management is an overt discriminatory technique since labor is restricted to less opulent "johns." In societies or communities where such direct and obvious techniques may violate certain democratic beliefs or norms, the covert methods are more frequent. In the United States, in the area of race relations, such techniques are numerous— use of grandfather clauses in voting restrictions, restricting apprentice programs in labor unions to sons of the present members, sending a black applicant for a job back and forth between departments until he gets discouraged, or filing a minority application for employment under "G" (for garbage).[6]

The last element which constitutes the meaning of the term "differential treatment" is *sanctions*. Sanctions are utilized to reward or to punish those who conform to the discriminatory norms or who attempt to violate them. Police can enforce the norms (in the American South, the police have been the major enforcers of violations of "racial etiquette") and courts can punish the offenders. Sanctions can take the form of "illegitimate" violence in the form of murder, destruction of property or beatings. Sanctions can, more commonly, consist of threats and disapproving behavior (e.g., in a tavern, ". . . put a head on their beer, serve them in a different glass to show you don't want them around, break the glass when they're finished").[7] A White Citizen's Council speaker stated, "We intend to make it difficult, if not impossible, for any Negro who advocates desegregation to find and hold a job, get credit, or renew a mortgage."[8] No system of discrimination could long endure, however, strictly on the basis of negative sanctions. Positive sanctions must accompany the negative. Subordinant statuses can enjoy paternalistic protection and care (women, children, slaves), financial rewards, extra privileges, social advancement, and social approval, if they cooperate. Sanctions are often invoked against individuals within the *dominant* category by other members of the position if they violate discriminatory norms. Legal proceedings, fines, scorn, ostracism, and noncooperation in business and social activities are common negative sanctions imposed on the dominant status member who offends.

Differential treatment involves norms, techniques, and sanctions. The last part of the definition deals with function of this treatment—the denying or restricting of the choices of a subordinant status. If freedom is defined as the maximization of choice, then discrimination negates in some degree one's freedom in a few or in many areas of social life. The areas of social life that have been restricted or denied to the varieties of discriminated statuses are numerous: occupations, residency, marriage, travel, membership in organizations, sexual activity, income, access to public facilities, and place of burial, to name a few (a more comprehensive and systematic list related to *racial* discrimination will be given in a later section of this chapter).

These restrictions should not be thought of simply as the *direct* result of a particular form of discriminatory treatment. Differential treatment in one specific area of social life cannot only affect this area, but the same treatment can have indirect effects on other areas. For example, discrimination which restricts one's educational attainment can also affect a number of other areas of social life, even if discrimination is absent in these—one's occupation, one's income, one's residency, etc. This is why a piecemeal or segmental attack on discrimination has little success because of the web of causal interconnections, and why only a *system* approach can produce effective results.

A major theoretical issue is involved in this concept of restrictive functions and can best be explained in terms of race relations. Is a technique *not* based upon a racially discriminatory norm but which, nevertheless, restricts the choices of members of a race to be called *racial* discrimination—for example, college board exams which are not designed to keep out blacks from a university, but function to do just this? In keeping with the theoretical perspective developed to this point, it will be argued that this is not racial discrimination. It may be class discrimination or discrimination against poor test-takers, but it is not racial discrimination. Certainly, racial discrimination is indirectly involved in this example, in terms of racial discrimination in schooling which functioned to produce low scores. The admissions test (where no racial norm exists) is not racial discrimination; racial discrimination is involved in the providing of inadequate and unequal public school resources. To mix these together under the term racial discrimination or "institutional racism" is to conceptually "muddy" an already confused area. Admittedly, some change in college admissions requirements *may* be necessary to reduce racial *inequality*, but racial inequality and racial discrimination are not synonomous terms (as will be examined more fully later in this chapter).

Before examining variations in discrimination generally, and the nature of racial discrimination, specifically, one further emphasis must be added. A norm or an institutionalized cluster of norms (an institution), however authoritarian in its restrictions on human choice and freedom, is *not* discrimination if it is not selective; that is, if the norms and their corresponding techniques and sanctions apply equally to everybody in the society, then there is no discrimination. Discrimination is *unequal* treatment where the advantages and privileges of some group or status are denied to another category.

Discrimination against any category of human beings varies in at least two important respects—the degree to which discrimination restricts choice and the number and type of exceptions that are made in this restriction. A category of human beings may be restricted to just one occupation or to several. They may be forced to convert to a particular religion or they may be allowed to follow any faith but their own. The total number of norms and the number of areas circumscribed can vary—hence many areas of social life can be restricted, or just a few. A black slave on a large plantation certainly had a much greater number of discriminatory norms imposed on him in a greater number of areas of life, with more severe sanctions imposed for violation, than had a Japanese–American in California in 1920. The duration of time that choice is restricted also relates to this important variation.

The other variation is the number of and type of categorical exceptions that are made or allowed by the dominant category. Individuals, or whole subcategories, are often exempted from discrimination for a variety of reasons depending upon the case in question. Professionals within an ethnic category are often exempted from discriminatory immigration norms. Upper-middle class black people may be allowed to move into all-white neighborhoods as long as their numbers are few. An exceptionally talented woman may be allowed into a profession that generally excludes females. Graduate students may be afforded greater privileges than undergraduate students. Or a house slave may be exempted from many of the more severe restrictions on behavior that are imposed on field slaves.

It is now necessary to put the concept of discrimination into a larger context which should help in further clarification—the larger context of social stratification.

Discrimination and Social Stratification

In the previous discussion of the nature of discrimination, it was emphasized that discrimination requires a social power differential. It is for this reason, along with the consequences of discrimination, that categorical restrictions may best be understood in the larger context of social stratification. In all complex societies, and in the organizations within these societies, an unequal distribution of power, privileges, prestige, and wealth exist in relationship to social positions and to social categories. Coexistent with this inequality, more or less differentiated life styles exist as well as differentiated life chances.[e] Discrimination is, or should be, a major concept in stratification analysis. Because of the differences in social power discrimination is possible, and, at the same time,

---

[e]Differentiated life styles relates to subcultural variations; life-chances may be defined as the varying probability of suffering some disadvantage or attaining some advantage.

discrimination is the major factor in maintaining and perpetuating differences in social power. In addition, discrimination limits social mobility (within positions in an organization or between classes in the society); discrimination helps to maintain social distance barriers to social interaction between positions and groups; discrimination, *in part*, functions to produce differences in life styles and life chances; discrimination creates and maintains differences in privileges, income, and education; and discrimination helps to create consciousness-of-kind within the dominant and within the subordinant categories.

With one exception[f], the causes and the effects of discrimination are directly related to stratification analysis. The causes of discrimination have been delineated by many theorists as (1) prejudice (categorical antipathy) due to status insecurity and to perceived competitive threats of other social categories; (2) the perception of advantage gained by restricting or denying the rights and privileges shared by one's own social category; and (3) conformity to the accepted social practices of one's own group. All of these are certainly intermeshed within systems of structured inequality. And, as has previously been mentioned, discrimination has, in part, functioned to maintain differences in power, privilege, income, education, and to maintain social distance barriers; it has also functioned to create, in part, differences in life styles and differences in the psychological, social, and cultural advantages and disadvantages that accrue to individuals within social systems. The causes of discrimination are understandable and best explained within the context of social stratification.

Racial Discrimination and Racial Stratification

Discrimination and social stratification have, so far, been examined generally. *Racial* discrimination is a particular type of discrimination where all of the above apply, with the symbolic category in question being race. Race, in the most common usage, refers to aggregates of people based upon physical differences, particularly skin color. Racial symbolic categories may be such common words as white, black, brown, red, yellow, oriental, or Indian (or gooks, flatheads, jigs, jungle-bunnies, honkies, etc.); or they may have more technical names such as Caucasoid, Mongoloid, Negroid, and Australoid. Categories such as Mexicans, Chinese, and Japanese, although technically ethnic groups,[g] may also be

---

[f]*Pathological* prejudice as a cause for a few discriminatory acts.

[g]Ethnic groups may be defined as peoples who conceive of themselves as kind by virtue of their common ancestry (real or imagined), who are united by emotional bonds, a common culture, and by concern with preservation of their group. (This is a slight modification of the definition by Tamotsu Shibutani and Kian Kwan.)[9]

considered as races in the United States because of highly identifiable physical differences. Since racial discrimination develops due to common meanings, the anthropological and biological meanings given to the word "race" are not relevant due to their limited currency. Racial discrimination may be defined as differential treatment by members of a dominant race which functions to deny or to restrict the choices of members of a subordinate race. Comparative examinations of patterns of racial discrimination reveal a large number of types of discrimination that make up a general classification of the specific norms and practices in particular societies. Included in the classification is the restriction on or denial of the following:

1. property use and ownership;
2. business practices;
3. membership in particular organizations (church, union, corporation, club, etc.);
4. occupancy of certain positions within an organization;
5. voting;
6. membership in particular occupations;
7. citizenship;
8. availability of community services (garbage removal, fire protection, street maintenance, enforcement of zoning and building codes, etc.);
9. religious belief and practice;
10. publishing and writing;
11. immigration into a society and migration within a society;
12. assembly and gathering (in terms of size of, place of, time of, and/or content of);
13. use of a language;
14. admittance to public or private buildings or upon the uses of the facilities available within these buildings;
15. sexual relations;
16. educational opportunity and quality of opportunity;
17. utilization of public transportation facilities;
18. legal rights in court cases;
19. police protection and protection from the police;
20. coverage in the mass media;
21. income or wages;
22. burial sites;
23. area of residency and quality of housing;
24. etiquette in interpersonal relations;
25. dress and personal appearance;
26. practicing of native customs (other than no. 9); and
27. one's presence in a community.

Racial stratification exists *within* the estate, class, or caste strata of the larger society and within the hierarchy of positions within particular organizations; it is not a special type that can be examined outside of these contexts. It may be said to exist when there is a disproportionate distribution of two or more races within the general stratification system of a multiracial society—a disproportionate distribution in terms of such factors as income, occupation, education, and positions of policy-making. This unequal distribution is primarily due to past and/or present discrimination, but may be due also to the adherence to cultural values, cultural beliefs, and forms of social organization that limit effective competitive ability (e.g., American Indians). Racial discrimination and racial inequality or stratification are not synonymous terms but analytically separate variables. Racial discrimination is the major independent variable that affects the degree of racial inequality, but it is not the only independent variable. As noted above, the other major independent variable that affects racial inequality is the degree of competitive ability. The higher distribution of Japanese-Americans in the stratification system as compared with Mexican-Americans is not due solely to differences in Anglo discrimination against these two groups. As will be examined in a later chapter, this distinction between racial discrimination and racial stratification has important implications for public policies.

Racial Discrimination and Related Concepts

Frequently associated with and often confused with racial discrimination, besides racial stratification, are several other concepts that must be analytically distinguished in any theoretical treatment of discrimination. The first of these is the concept of prejudice. Prejudice has many meanings as used by social scientists—it has been defined as an attitude *and/or* behavior, as essentially irrational thinking or as rational *and* irrational, as abnormal *and* normal, and as a positive or a negative attitude *or* just as a negative attitude. The majority of social scientists who use this word, however, define it as an attitude, as a negative attitude, and as a negative attitude directed towards a whole category. But prejudice defined simply as an attitude raises certain problems. A male driver who yells out of his car window at a female driver, "You stupid broad" is certainly demonstrating prejudice, but this is behavior and not just a "predisposition to behavior" (attitude). This book will define prejudice as the degree of behavioral *and* attitudinal antipathy directed against an entire symbolic category or against an individual within a category solely because the individual is a member of the category. More simply, prejudice is *categorical antipathy*. The degree to·which this antipathy directed against a whole category is realistic or the degree to which the categorical antipathy is normative are two analytically separate variables that must be examined as they relate to particular instances of prejudice. They need not be made a part of the meaning of prejudice. The relationship between prejudice and discrimination is not necessarily a causal one. *One* major cause of discrimination is prejudice; however, other causes of discrimination exist as have been pointed out, and it is possible to discriminate and not be prejudiced. In addition, it is possible to be prejudiced and not to discriminate. To discriminate one must have the social power to do so. It is one thing to hurl epithets and quite another to prevent the social mobility of a subordinant group. In situations where discrimination is *negatively* sanctioned by significant others, most prejudiced individuals will conform to a nondiscriminatory policy in spite of any feelings or attitudes of categorical antipathy (e.g., a white clerk serving a black in a store where overt prejudicial statements and behavior and where discriminatory acts are grounds for dismissal).

A second concept related to discrimination to racial groups is segregation. This concept may simply be defined as *spatial separation* and is one form of a more inclusive concept—social distance. The existence of segregation does not necessarily imply the existence of discrimination; segregation may be voluntarily created and maintained. Many European ethnic minorities voluntarily segregated themselves into areas of American cities, and today, most Indians want to maintain their segregated reservation systems. Even American black segregation is not entirely nonvoluntary. If, however, segregation is imposed on a group by another race or ethnic group, then this type of segregation is a form of discrimination.

The last concept that is frequently associated with or confused with racial discrimination is racism. In recent years, this word has taken on a bewildering variety of meanings. It has meant racial discrimination, racial prejudice, racial stratification, the disproportionate latent effects on a race due to class discrimination and/or inequality, and the doctrine of racial inferiority and superiority. In some recent works, the term has become a generic word to subsume all of these meanings.[10] It is suggested here, that the word, "racism," be limited to the doctrine of racial inferiority and superiority. This has been its major historical meaning, and we already have the other concepts in our verbal baggage.

Keeping the word, racism, to this meaning, it is possible to ask some very interesting theoretical questions that need empirical examination: Do forms of racial discrimination exist that are not legitimated by racism; can one believe in racism and not racially discriminate; does the existence of racism precede and cause the formation of racial discrimination and racial stratification, or is racism an ideological effect of racial stratification that is used to legitimate an established set of discriminatory practices, etc.?

With this attempt to clarify the concept of discrimination generally and the concept of racial discrimination in particular, certain research problems present themselves:

1. What is the extent of formal and informal discriminatory norms in particular organizations and in particular communities today?
2. What kinds of discriminatory techniques are being utilized, if any, in particular organizations and in particular communities?
3. How is it possible to measure the degree of effectiveness of racial discrimination? The degree to which a discriminatory norm is adhered to by members of a dominant race and subordinant race? The reasons why members of a subordinant race do not challenge the norms? The degree of success of the intent of the norm (e.g., voting rates)? The number of times a norm is violated and sanctions are imposed?
4. Is it possible to find two similar communities where the difference in discrimination is great and thereby be able to ascertain the effect of discrimination on inequality, as opposed to other factors?
5. Is it possible to ascertain a pattern of sequential effects of racial discrimination in one area upon other areas?
6. Are beliefs such as racism major determinants of racial discrimination or are they *post hoc* legitimations of racial discrimination? Or is there some particular pattern of interaction between these two variables?
7. How can a social scientist ascertain the existence of and the extent of covert discriminatory techniques and informal discriminatory norms? Survey techniques seem to be highly inadequate in this type of research; possibly only the technique of participant observer would be effective.
8. Is the common practice of using data of racial inequality (e.g., occupational distribution, membership rates, unemployment rates, educational attainment, etc.) as proof of the existence of racial discrimination a valid procedure? What other factors could produce this inequality?
9. Does the significance of racial prejudice in affecting racial discrimination vary according to specific social situations or types of social activities? For example, is prejudice more of a causal factor in affecting discriminatory behavior in relatively unstructured social situations and social activities, as opposed to highly structured social conditions?
10. What is the effect of racial inequality upon racial discrimination (as opposed to the other way around)? For example, does discrimination lessen as a group achieves greater proportional representation in the stratification system?

11. Do discriminatory norms which are covert and informal become overt and formal when a minority race enters areas of social life which they have never previously entered? Do discriminatory norms emerge where there were none previously when this occurs? Do formal overt norms change to informal and covert when a minority race increases its challenges to these norms?

The major research problem involved in this whole area of racial discrimination, racial stratification, and racial public policies is the problem of ascertaining the extent of and type of discrimination that exists in particular areas—geographical and social. Ascertaining the degree of prejudice is relatively easy compared with this. Until this can be done, such relationships of discrimination with inequality, discrimination with prejudice, discrimination with segregation, and discrimination with racism will always be inadequate. If we cannot ascertain or measure the degree to which discrimination varies in terms of time and place, we cannot examine how other factors affect or are affected by this variation.

2

Historical Summary of Black Discrimination and Black-White Stratification in the United States

The Formative Period: 1510-1700

In the fifteenth, sixteenth and seventeenth centuries, several advanced kingdoms existed in West Africa—the major ones being the kingdoms of Mali, Benin, Kongo, Songhay, Dahomey, Loango, Angola, Oyo, Adansi, Hausa, Akan, Akwamu, and Denkyira. European traders first made contact with these kingdoms when in 1462 the Portuguese broke the Arab monopoly on the sale of blacks by bringing the first black slaves to the Iberian peninsula. This trade became so intensive that by 1518 the southern portion of Portugal south of Lisbon was predominantly black. In 1510, the Great Circuit began when the Spanish monarch gave orders for the transport of 200 slaves to the West Indies. By 1592, a new license was issued by the Spanish government for the transport of 38,250 slaves. The Great Circuit involved the export of cheap manufactured goods from Europe to Africa, primarily weapons; the purchase or seizure of slaves on the Guinea coast and their transportation across the Atlantic to first the West Indies and then later to North and South America; and the exchange of these slaves for minerals and foodstuffs which were then transported and sold in Europe. In these contacts of Europeans with the black kingdoms of Africa, the European captains and traders went ashore, whether for trade or for warlike expeditions against other European rivals, in agreement with this or that coastal chief or king; it was not a simple case of white conquerors vs. primitive blacks. Pushed, however, by their desire for European goods or blackmailed by the fear that what one or two might refuse, their rivals would consent to give, the rulers of Africa surrendered to the slave trade. The slave trade became inseparable from chiefly rule. Wherever the trade found strong chiefs and kings, it prospered almost from the first; wherever it failed to find them, it caused them to come into being. Individuals from such ethnic groups as the Mandingo, Nupe, Yoruba, Susu, Bambara, Tuculor, Fulani, Kissi, Senufu, and Ibo were ruthlessly subjugated and transported across the sea where it has been estimated that approximately half of them died in the middle passage.[1]

In the early colonies in what is now the eastern United States, the first black immigrants fell into a well-established socioeconomic position that carried no implication of racial inferiority. For approximately 40 years, black and white immigrants mingled on the basis of substantial equality within the indentured

15

servant class. Blacks had social privileges equal to those accorded white servants and widespread intermingling occurred in terms of both marriage and sexual relations outside of marriage.[2] Within a short period as the Great Circuit increased in volume, blacks and slavery became synonymous, and between 1660 and 1700, laws were passed in most of the colonies making black slaves, slaves for life; intermarriage was prohibited, and the children born of black women were ruled bond or free according to the status of the mother. By 1765, all of the Southern states had miscegenation laws.[3]

Institutionalized Discrimination in the South: 1700-1865

Between the years 1700 and 1750, a severe caste system of discriminatory norms had become institutionalized into law and custom. The following are the major norms of southern slavery as summarized from Stampp and Elkins (and put into present tense):[4]

1. Constraints on marriage and sexual relations.[5]
   a. Slaves cannot marry free Negroes.
   b. Marriage between slaves has no standing in law.
   c. The father of a Negro child is legally unknown (without this law there would have been the creation of a free mulatto class, since many of the fathers were white planters).
   d. Children of slaves can be separated from their parents and sold separately.
   e. Sexual relations between male slaves and white females is prohibited; sexual relations between white masters and slave females is acceptable.

2. Constraints on movement.[6]
   a. Slaves are not to be out of their cabins after eight o'clock in the winter and nine o'clock in the summer.
   b. Slaves cannot leave the estate without a pass giving the destination and time of returning.
   c. Slaves cannot be on the streets of towns and cities after curfew (6:00).

3. Constraints on ownership of property.[7]
   a. Slaves cannot own property except at the will and pleasure of the master.
   b. Slaves cannot keep cattle, horses, hogs, mules, or sheep (masters who permit this will be fined by the courts).
   c. A slave cannot own a book, possess weapons, purchase liquor, receive gifts, make a will, or inherit anything.

4. Restrictions on interpersonal behavior.[8]
   a. Slaves must respect all white men and show absolute obedience to their masters.
   b. A slave cannot raise his hand against a white man nor use insulting or abusive language.
   c. Slaves must step out of the way when a white person approaches.
   d. Slaves cannot beat drums or blow horns.
   e. In Charleston, slaves cannot swear, smoke, walk with a cane, or ride in a carriage except as a menial (city ordinance).
   f. Slaves cannot gamble with whites or with other slaves.

5. Constraints on assembly.[9]
   a. Any gathering of more than five slaves away from home and unattended by a white is unlawful assembly—regardless of purpose or orderly decorum.
   b. Washington and North Carolina: Slaves and free Negroes are not permitted to assemble in the streets, markets, or other public places.
   c. Charleston: Negroes cannot assemble at parades or other joyful demonstrations.

6. Constraints on education and on religious belief and practice.[10]
   a. Slaves (and in some states free Negroes) cannot learn to read or write.
   b. No slave can be employed in a printing office.
   c. No slave can preach except on his master's premise and in the presence of whites.
   d. No Negro ministry is allowed.
   e. Religious instruction to be done only by the master or with his permission.
   f. South Carolina: No religious meetings of slaves or free Negroes are allowed either before the rising of the sun or after.

7. Constraints on occupational positions.[11]
   a. Slaves are limited only to the duties as defined by masters.
   b. Slaves cannot hire their own time nor find their own employment.

8. Restrictions on political participation and on rights in court.[12]
   a. Slaves are not citizens and cannot vote.
   b. Negroes, free of slave, cannot testify in court against a white man.
   c. A slave is not a competent witness except in a case involving another slave.
   d. Whites accused of murdering a slave are not to be convicted (informal norm, with exceptions).
   e. Minor offenses of slaves are not to be tried in courts that also try whites,

but they are to be tried, convicted, and punished on the plantation. (Capital offenses are to be tried in regular courts.)

A variety of both positive and negative sanctions were utilized by the white dominant group to enforce this caste system of discriminatory norms. On the large plantations, modern methods of crushing resistance were utilized, involving constant fatigue, insecurity, and overwhelming power over life and death.[13] Generally, the goal was to "... accustom him to rigid discipline, demand from him unconditional submission, impress upon him his innate inferiority, develop in him a paralyzing fear of white men, train him to adopt the master's code of good behavior, and instill in him a sense of complete dependence."[14] The slave role was expected to involve such attributes as obedience, fidelity, humility, docility, and cheerfulness (also important virtues for dogs and children). There was no role for the slave father; he had no authority over children, he could not protect the mother of his children except by appeal to his master. The role of the master was one of paternalism: he must be wise, just, and authoritative and prepared to cope with his children who though often obedient could be lazy, silly, irresponsible and dishonest.[15] The specific negative sanctions that were most commonly utilized were: whipping, demotion to field labor, threatening the slave with being sold, deprivation of food, forced work on Sundays and holidays, use of private jails and stocks, use of chains and irons, branding and mutilation, outlawing runaways, and execution or murder.[16] Positive sanctions involved money rewards, granting of a small plot of land for slave use, profit-sharing agreements, gifts at Christmas, time off from duties for good behavior, and the observing of special holidays other than Christmas.[17]

This "total" institution was legitimated by racism and by religion. Scientists, doctors, politicians, theologians, and other "experts" (particularly in the nineteenth century) developed racist thinking into a highly detailed ideological system.[18] In this system, blacks were an inferior race, whether viewed from a religious viewpoint or from an evolutionary one, and it was slavery that raised the black from barbarism: "Slavery has done more to elevate a degraded race in the scale of humanity, to tame the savage, to civilize the barbarous, to soften the ferocious, to enlighten the ignorant, and to spread the blessings of Christianity among the heathen than all the missionaries that philanthropy and religion have ever sent forth."[19]

Institutionalized Discrimination in the North: 1700-1865

With only about 10 percent of the total American black population residing in the North until the beginning of the twentieth century, along with the relative absence of large plantations, the conditions of the free black and the slave black were somewhat better than in the South. Within the North, before the virtual abolition of slavery around 1800, conditions also varied. New England was the most favorable social climate for blacks, while the middle colonies (and later middle states), particularly New Jersey and New York, were the most restrictive. Because of considerable variation by state, it is not possible to make up a list of discriminatory norms applicable to the entire North; however, the following is a list that while not exhaustive, does illustrate this variation.

1. Constraints on movement.[20]
   a. The entrance of Negroes into this state will be prohibited or restricted. Nearly every northern state considers, and many adopt, measures to prohibit or restrict the further immigration of Negroes.[21] Most new states, particularly in the Northwest Territory (northwest in early 1800s) bar Negroes explicitly or permit them to enter only after they have produced certified proof of their freedom and post a bond, ranging from $500 to $1,000 which would guarantee their good behavior. Delaware in 1851 prohibits the immigration of free Negroes from any state except Maryland. Indiana in 1851 prohibits free Negroes from coming into the state and fines all persons who encourage them to remain in the state between $10 and $500 for each offense. Oregon in 1849 forbids entrance of Negroes.
   b. Indians or Negroes (free or slave) cannot be on the streets at night, with violators to be punished by whipping (Rhode Island, 1703).

2. Constraints relating to criminal procedures and court actions.[22]
   a. Slave testimony allowed only in cases of slave conspiracies (almost all Northern states).
   b. Slaves are to receive more severe punishment than nonslaves for capital crimes (all Northern states).
   c. Slaves are to be tried in special courts (only in New York and New Jersey).
   d. Negroes cannot make contracts or maintain lawsuits (Oregon).
   e. Negroes cannot provide testimony in cases where a white man was a party (Illinois, Ohio, Indiana, Iowa, and California). Because of this lack of legal protection, a white can assault, rob, or even murder a Negro in the midst of a number of Negro witnesses and escape prosecution unless another white man had been present and had agreed to testify.[23]
   f. Negroes are to be excluded from jury service.

3. Restrictions on citizenship and voting.[24]
   a. Naturalization is to be limited to white aliens only (passed by Congress in 1790).
   b. Negroes are not citizens and can therefore claim none of the rights and

privileges that the Constitution guarantees citizens (Dred Scott decision). This decision merely confirms existing state and federal practices sanctioned by both major political parties.[25]

c. Negroes cannot vote in elections. "From the admission of Maine in 1819 until the end of the Civil War, every new state restricted suffrage to whites in its constitution."[26] In New Jersey and Connecticut, the original constitutions have no racial restrictions but suffrage is limited by the legislature and subsequent new constitutions incorporate the restrictions. In New York only, blacks require a property qualification to vote—must own at least $250 worth of estate; and as late as 1869 New York voters defeat any proposals to grant equal suffrage to Negroes.

4. Constraints on membership in organizations.[27]
   a. Negroes cannot belong to state militias (Congress, 1792).
   b. Negroes cannot carry the United States mail (Congress, 1810).
   c. Negroes cannot enlist in the Marines or for service on naval warships (Departments of War and Navy edicts in 1798; not enforced, however).

5. Constraints on Assembly.[28]
   a. Negroes cannot attend camp meetings, except for religious worship under the control of white people (Delaware, 1851).
   b. More than three slaves cannot meet unless authorized by white authorities; punishment to consist of 40 lashes on the bare back (New York, 1702).
   c. Negroes cannot meet in groups (Pennsylvania).

6. Restrictions on property ownership.[29]
   a. Slaves and free Negroes cannot own land (New York).
   b. New York and New Jersey (only northern states to do so) Negroes cannot own property of any kind (eliminated in New York in 1730 and in New Jersey after the Revolutionary War).
   c. Negroes cannot own real estate (Oregon).

7. Restrictions on quality and availability of education.[30]
   a. Negroes are not to receive formalized education or they must receive education in segregated schools. ". . . Most northern states either excluded them altogether or established separate schools for them. . . . In New England, local school committees usually assigned Negro children to separate institutions, regardless of the district in which they resided. Pennsylvania and Ohio, although extending their public school privileges to all children, required district school directors to establish separate facilities for Negro students whenever twenty or more could be accom-

modated.... The new states frequently excluded Negroes from all public education, but by 1850, most of them consented to separate instruction.... By the 1830s statute or custom placed Negro children in separate schools in nearly every northern community."[31]

    b. Public funds for Negro schools and for Negro teachers' salaries shall be less than for white schools and white teachers' salaries.

8. Restrictions and constraints on admission, seating and service in public buildings and accommodations.[32]

    a. Negroes cannot enter hotels, restaurants, or resorts except as servants.

    b. Negroes must be segregated in public accommodations—railway cars, stagecoaches, steamboats.

    c. Negroes must sit in special sections in churches (African corner or Nigger pews, or B.M.—black members).

    d. Negroes must sit in special sections (secluded and remote) in theatres, lecture halls.

Woodward gives an excellent summary of the discrimination and racism in the North before the Civil War: "... the Northern Negro was made painfully and constantly aware that he lived in a society dedicated to the doctrine of white supremacy and Negro inferiority. The major political parties, whatever their position on slavery, vied with each other in their devotion to this doctrine, and extremely few politicians of importance dared question them.... They made sure in numerous ways that the Negro understood his place and was severely confined to it."[33]

Transformation and Formation, 1865-1900:
Reconstruction and Reaction

With the elimination of slavery (13th Amendment, 1865), the South went through a period of confused, conflicting, and inconsistent behavior until 1900 when a new system developed and became institutionalized—*apartheid*. During this period, it was not evident just what new patterns would emerge as conflicting forces operated. Almost immediately after the war, most Southern states passed legislation that would virtually put the black back into slavery (the black codes). Reacting to these laws, the Republican Congress passed the first Reconstruction Act in 1867 which placed the South under military occupation. This was followed by the 14th Amendment (due process under the law), the 15th Amendment (voting rights), and finally by the Civil Rights Act of 1875 (which made illegal discrimination in public accommodations and public facilities such as inns and theatres and discrimination in jury selection).

Various forces vied with each other in this period, all of which would have had significant effects on race relations if successful. The Bourbons or aristocrats wanted a class system dominated by themselves but with no segregation or humiliation of blacks. A growing Populist movement emphasized a united black and white proletariat to change the class system. A minority of liberals advocated equality. And finally, a significant segment demanded the subordination of the black. By the 1890s, the Bourbons had been discredited due to the depressions of the 1880s, by their alliance with Northern industrialists, and by their unpopular Hamiltonian views of finance. The Populist movement lost momentum, and the white populists turned against their black allies, blaming them for the failure of their agrarian reforms. The liberals, north and south, deserted the black cause, wrote racist articles, and became convinced that the divided country could only be united by making the black the scapegoat. The racist position emerged triumphant, and the whites would no longer be divided by appealing to the black vote.[34]

Before this triumph of racism and the establishment of apartheid, ". . . in most parts of the South . . . race relations during Reconstruction could not be said to have crystalized or stabilized nor to have become what they later became. There were too many cross currents and contradictions, revolutionary innovations and violent reactions."[35] It was a period of role confusion between the races, a period of increased competition and conflict, and a period of self-conscious and strained behavior. From about 1870 to around 1900, there was no generally accepted code of racial mores.[36]

Discrimination and inequality was less in this period than during slavery and during the period 1900-1940. Blacks voted, took their places on juries, were elected to legislative bodies, and in many places, mingled with whites in public facilities and accommodations. Black leaders organized sit-ins, walk-ins, and ride-ins to force implementation of the new antidiscrimination policies of the federal government and of the new state constitutions of the South. Black workers improved their class position by infiltrating the building trades industry and other skilled occupations. At the same time, many white farmers sifted down to the class level of the black rural laborers.[37]

It should be emphasized that this was not a golden age of race relations in America. In many areas of the South, old patterns of relationships persisted and new patterns of violence and exploitation occurred. But it was a different period. As Woodward has stated, ". . . it would be a mistaken effort to equate this period in racial relations with either the old regime of slavery or with the future role of Jim Crow. It was too exceptional."[38]

In 1877, the federal troops were withdrawn from the South, and with the weakening of the other positions, the position of extreme racism and segregation gradually grew in influence. This new pattern was indicated in a variety of ways.

"Lynchings in the South increased rapidly from 1882 up to 1890, and showed a further sharp rise in the early nineties when the white South began to legislate the subordination of the Negro; the downward trend thereafter coincided with the growing tendency on his part to accept, at least outwardly, the status forced upon him."[39] The 1888 census data on occupations indicated that white workers were increasing their proportions in skilled occupations in the building trades, occupations in which the blacks formerly held important positions.[40] In 1883, the Supreme Court declared the Civil Rights Bill of 1875 unconstitutional and in 1896 declared school segregation legal as long as it was equal. These decisions paved the way for the formation of segregated schools and segregated public accommodations which rapidly spread throughout the South in the period 1895-1905. The growth of poll taxes, white primaries, and literacy tests, accompanied by violence and intimidation, rapidly disenfranchised the black voter. A major example of these forms of discrimination and their effectiveness was in Louisiana. In 1896, there were 130,334 registered black voters; by 1904, there were only 1,342; black registrants were a majority in 26 parishes in 1896, but by 1900 there were no parishes with a black majority.[41]

A new system had been born in the South (with many elements of continuity from the old system, of course, but a new system nevertheless). This "edifice of white supremacy was virtually completed by 1906."[42] It now "became a punishable offense against the laws or the mores for whites and Negroes to travel, eat, defecate, wait, be buried, make love, play, relax, and even speak together, except in the stereotyped context of master and servant inter-action."[43]

Stabilization of Dominance, 1900-1945:
Apartheid, Southern Style

Slavery was a caste system based upon the idea of chattel property. The patterns of discrimination and dominance-subordination that now had crystallized were no less a caste system. Three distinguished scholars did extensive studies of discrimination in the South in the 1930s and early 1940s—Charles S. Johnson, Gunnar Myrdal, and John Dollard. The following is a composite summary of their findings, again utilizing the normative conception developed in Chapter 2.

1. Restrictions on occupational employment, mobility, and union member-ship.[44]
   a. Negroes are to be restricted to the least desirable occupations—to those not desired by white workers.
   b. Negro professionals, white collar employees, and merchants are to serve only other Negroes.

    c. Negroes are to receive lower pay for the same work. "When there were technical innovations, making work less strenuous, less dirty, and generally more attractive, this often implied a redefinition of the occupations from 'Negro jobs' to 'white man's work' ".[45]

    d. When unemployment or periods of work stoppage develops Negroes shall be the first to be discharged.

    e. Membership in unions by Negroes is not permitted or they must be segregated locals. "In general, labor organizations in all but a few of the southern and border states either exclude or segregate the races. . . . The exceptions to this rule are significant, however, and represent fields in which Negro workers have become fairly well entrenched as, for example, in mining, in iron and steel manufacturing, and in slaughtering and meat packing."[46]

The labor unions (North and South) that exclude all Negroes by special clauses in their constitutions or rituals: locomotive engineers; aeronautical workers; railway car men; railway and steamship clerks; railway express-men; trainmen and firemen; train dispatchers; yard masters; master's mates and pilots; switchmen; railroad telegraphers; railway mail clerks; dining-car conductors; sleeping car conductors; railroad station employees; wire weavers; boilermakers; machinists; commercial telegraphers. Unions which exclude Negroes completely as a matter of custom, but without exclusion clauses in their constitutions: plumbers, electrical workers, rural letter carriers; flint-glass workers. Unions which expressly prohibit racial discrimination: ministers, teachers, ladies garment makers; fur workers; subway construction workers; employees of maritime shipping agencies, automobile manufacturing, and rubber fabrication.[47]

2. Restrictions or constraints on educational quality and availability.[48]

    a. Negro students are to be segregated from white students.

    b. Negro teachers are to receive less pay than white teachers. The average annual salary for teachers in Negro schools in 17 southern states during 1935-6 was $510 compared with $833 for teachers in white schools in the same states and year.

    c. Public monies allocated to schools should be predominately distributed to white schools. "In the seventeen states receiving sixteen million dollars for Negro and white land-grant colleges in 1935-6 Negroes constituted 25 percent of the total population between the ages of 18 and 21 inclusive; yet they received only 5.4 percent of the total federal allotments."[49] Racial discrimination in the apportionment of school facilities in the South is as spectacular as it is well known."[50] Since state appropriations are on a per capita basis, in counties where Negroes are the majority, discrimination in appropriation means considerably more money for white students.

d. Negro pupils and teachers are to be excluded from access to the equipment used by the white children and by the white teaching staff.

e. Craft and vocational training are to be given black students and not other forms of higher education; a complete four-year high school course for Negroes is not necessary. In 12 states having separate schools for Negroes, there were 115 counties in 1938-9 that did not provide four-year courses in the separate high schools. ". . . there appears to be substantial support for the contention that a large proportion of the Negroes of high school age who are not in school are in that category because of the lack of high-school facilities in the counties where they live."[51]

3. Restraints on voting.[52]

a. Registration requirements are to be stringently enforced for Negroes than for whites. In 1944, seven states had poll taxes. ". . . election officials practically always demand to see the poll tax receipts of Negroes and seldom those of whites."[53] Educational requirements exist in 7 southern states. "Relatively seldom is a white man 'insulted' by being given the test; yet many cases have been recorded where a Negro 'failed' the test when he mispronounced a single word."[54]

b. Negroes should be discouraged as potential voters. Various techniques are: "What do you want here, nigger?"; ignoring the prospective registrant; "We're all out of cards"; "All the members of the board are not present"; "We will notify you when it is time to register"; "losing" the Negro's card; "forgetting" to put his name on the list of voters; threats from newspapers about voting; threats from whites hanging around the polls. In the town studied by Dollard, he found that "it is possible for any one of the 9,000 in the white caste to vote if he complies with the stipulations; it is virtually impossible for any of the 24,000 in the Negro caste to vote no matter what their qualifications."[55]

4. Restrictions on rights in court trials and in police treatment.[56]

a. The word of a policeman must always be taken against any Negro witness or defendant in a court trial.

b. Negro testimony is to be given less credence than white testimony.

c. Suspected Negroes may be given harsher treatment than suspected whites (Negroes in the upper classes excepted).

d. The powers of Negro policemen are to be restricted.

e. Negroes should be excluded from jury duty (in serious cases involving Negroes where an appeal might be made because of the Scottsboro decision, some Negroes are selected).

f. Negroes are to receive more severe punishment for offenses against whites (as compared with the same offense committed by a white against a white).

5. Restrictions and constraints upon admission, seating, and service in public accommodations and buildings.[57]

a. Negroes must be separated from whites in all public forms of land transportation and Negro sections do not require the amount of maintenance and quality of accommodations as do the white sections. Missouri and West Virginia do not have laws requiring separation on trains; Kentucky and Maryland do not require separation on streetcars.

b. Negroes are not to be sold accommodations in Pullman cars.

c. Negroes (in Deep South) are to be excluded from public parks. (Johnson found that in Richmond, Virginia, Negroes could enter parks but were restricted to walking, sitting, and fishing; in Houston they could visit the zoo in one park on special days.)[58]

d. Negroes (in Border States) may enter and generally use parks, except they must use separate play facilities—swimming pools, tennis courts, playground equipment.

e. Negroes are not to use public libraries. "In 1939 it was found that of 774 public libraries in 13 Southern states only 99, or less than one-seventh, served Negroes. Of the 99 libraries, 59 were concentrated in four states (Virginia, Kentucky, Texas and North Carolina).[59] In some larger cities of the Deep South separate black libraries existed, but these were inadequately staffed with books.

f. Negroes are not to be admitted to private hospitals; emergency care may be given but only in segregated facilities.

g. Negroes may enter governmental buildings, but they must not loiter; they must remove their hats, and they must not expect service until all whites have been accommodated.

h. In courts, Negroes must sit in specially reserved sections (back or side).

i. No Negroes are to be accommodated in any hotel that receives white patronage. Hotel management may permit mixed meetings of organizations, but Negroes must use the side doors, the freight elevators, and must not loiter in the lobby.

j. Negroes may purchase goods in department stores, but they may not try on clothing or use the public lavatory facilities.

k. Negroes are to be excluded from swimming pools, skating rinks, bowling alleys, and dance halls where whites patronize. In motion picture theatres they must sit in the balcony or some other segregated section.

6. Restrictions and constraints on forms of interpersonal relations (Race Etiquette).[60]
   a. In doctor offices white patients are to be served first.
   b. No interracial dining is to be permitted (Negroes eat in Negro restaurants or come into white restaurants through the rear and eat in the kitchen).
   c. Negro employees must not interrupt the employer when he is talking with whites and must wait until all whites have finished with the employer.
   d. Negroes may not make social calls on whites.
   e. Negroes must take off their hats in the presence of whites; whites are not to take off theirs. (Negro men are expected to remove their hats if white women are present, but white men are not expected to remove theirs if only Negro women are present).
   f. Negroes are to enter white homes on service calls only through the back door; whites go through the front door into black homes. White men need show no sign of respect to Negroes in the Negro homes (such as knocking, removing hat, or standing when a Negro woman enters); these signs of respect must be shown by Negroes.
   g. A white man may offer his hand to a Negro for handshaking, but Negroes are not to make the gesture first.
   h. Sexual relations between black men and white women are absolutely forbidden (sexual relations between white men and black women are to be tolerated).
   i. Negroes, when driving an automobile, must always give white drivers and white pedestrians the right of way (Police officers enforce this norm by arresting Negro drivers on charges of reckless driving),
   j. Negro men are not to look up at white women sitting on their porches as they walk by.

7. Burial and death practices.[61]
   Negroes are not to be buried in the same cemetary as whites.

8. Restrictions on membership in organizations.[62]
   a. Negroes, with few exceptions, are not to be admitted into white *voluntary* associations.
   b. Negroes are not to be admitted into white *professional* organizations.

9. Restrictions on residency. Negroes must live in the special sections of towns and cities that are reserved for them and must not attempt to move into exclusive white areas.[63] This norm in the South took the form of zoning ordinances and/or restrictive covenants. When, in 1941, the Supreme Court

declared racial zoning ordinances unconstitutional, the primary emphasis was on restrictive covenants. When this in turn was declared unenforceable in the courts in 1948 by the Supreme Court the more informal techniques that had coexisted with these formal techniques became the method of implementing housing discrimination. A major informal technique was the simple expedient of real estate firms to not handle any transactions with Negroes involving housing in white neighborhoods. The Federal Housing Administration supported housing discrimination from 1935 to 1950. It's *Underwriting Manual* stated: "If a neighborhood is to retain stability, it is necessary that properties shall continue to be occupied by the same social and racial group." The FHA recommended that this model restrictive covenant be included in all property deeds.[64]

In this period, the police were the major enforcers of these discriminatory norms. They had strong support and help from the many white organizations who enforced discriminatory norms relevant to their specific organizations. But, probably the major factor that produced a highly effective discriminatory system was what Dollard called the "atmosphere of intimidation."

Every Negro in the South knows that he is under a kind of sentence of death; he does not know when his turn will come, it may never come, but it may also be at any time. This fear tends to intimidate the Negro man. If he loves his family, this love itself is a barrier against any open attempt to change his status. . . . Southern white people do not like to believe they have created such an uncomfortable situation for the Negro and are likely to minimize the fact. They tend to rely on the openly ascertained statistics of lynching and violence and to point out that not many Negroes are killed; what the white caste does not take into account is the emotional climate that is established for the Negro by asocial violence and by the many aggressive pressures which are leveled against him whenever he tries to claim his full status as a man in the sense of the wider American conception of a human being. What matters is the fear of extralegal violence, not knowing when or how the danger may appear, not being able to organize oneself with reference to it, uncertainty, and the mist of anxiety raised under such conditions.[65]

The North: 1860-1945

Little systematic work has been done on the black in the North between the years following the Civil War and the turn of the century. Most studies have been concerned with Reconstruction problems in the South during this period. Allan H. Spear[66] has written an excellent study dealing with Chicago from 1890-1920; however, he does give us some insight about conditions *prior* to 1890. Race relations in other Northern cities were probably similar.

By 1860, almost a thousand Negroes lived in Chicago. A small leadership group, headed by a well-to-do tailor, John Jones, participated in antislavery activities and articulated the grievances of a people who already found themselves the victims of segregation and discrimination.

Despite the presence of an active antislavery movement, Negroes in antebellum Chicago were severely circumscribed. Residents of downstate Illinois frequently characterized Chicago as a "sinkhole of abolition" and a "niggerloving town"; yet the sympathy that many white Chicagoans expressed for the Southern slaves was not often extended to the local Negroes. To be sure, the antislavery press, on occasion, noted approvingly the orderliness and respectability of the city's Negro community, but little was done to improve the status of the group. Chicago's Negroes could not vote, nor could they testify in court against whites. State law forbade intermarriage between the races. Segregation was maintained in the schools, places of public accommodation, and transportation. Chicago's abolitionists regarded these conditions as side issues and manifested little interest in them.

Between 1870 and 1890, the Chicago Negro community grew from less than four thousand to almost fifteen thousand and developed a well-delineated class structure and numerous religious and secular organizations. After the fire of 1871, the community became more concentrated geographically. Most Negroes lived on the South Side, but were still well interspersed with whites. . . . During the postwar years, the formal pattern of segregation that had characterized race relations in antebellum Chicago broke down. By 1870, Negroes could vote. In 1874, the school system was desegregated. A decade later, after the federal civil rights bill was nullified by the United States Supreme Court, the Illinois legislature enacted a law prohibiting discrimination in public places. Despite these advances, however, the status of Negroes in Chicago remained ambiguous. They continued to face discrimination in housing, employment, and, even in the face of the civil rights law, public accommodations. But they were not confined to a ghetto. Most Negroes, although concentrated in certain sections of the city, lived in mixed neighborhoods. Negro businessmen and professional men frequently catered to a white market and enjoyed social, as well as economic, contacts with the white community. And, although Negro churches and social clubs proliferated, there were still few separate civic institutions. . . . Generally ignored by white Chicagoans, Negroes were viewed neither as a threat to the city's well-being nor as an integral part of the city's social structure.[67]

As in the South, the period from 1890 to 1910 (or 1920 depending on the area) marked a new period in northern race relations and formed a relatively new system of racial discrimination. This new pattern in the North was produced by the increased migration of rural Southern blacks to Northern urban centers beginning around 1890 and increasing rapidly during the years of World War I. This migration pattern again accelerated during World War II. In 1900, 90% of all blacks lived in the South; and in 1940, 77%; by 1960, only 53.6% of blacks lived in the South. During these years, six states in the North and West absorbed 72% of these migrants—California, Illinois, Michigan, New York, Ohio, and Pennsylvania. Chicago's black population rose from 6,480 in 1880 to 44,103 in

1910 and to 109,458 ten years later. This was a percentage increase relative to whites in Chicago from 1.1 of whites in 1880 to 4.1% of whites in 1920.[68] This migration produced a new *competitive* pattern of race relations marked by competition over jobs, racial violence, the creation and the expansion of ghettos, the growth of restrictive covenants in real estate, increased discrimination in black access to public facilities, and the development of parallel black institutions.

Primarily utilizing Spear's work on Chicago and Myrdal's *American Dilemma*, the following discriminatory norms were established or reasserted in most Northern cities (New England was the major exception where discrimination was least against blacks in the United States):

1. Restrictions on housing and residency.[69]
   a. Negroes must live in their traditional areas of the city and should not attempt to move into white neighborhoods. If Negroes attempted this, and they did, whites attempted to buy up the property, utilized violence, and formed neighborhood protective associations (e.g., The Hyde Park Improvement Club in 1908) which used threats against real estate brokers who violated this norm. Restrictive covenants made their appearance in Chicago in 1927, and this technique rapidly spread throughout the city.
   b. Higher rents and less maintenance of property rented to Negroes by whites is acceptable practice.
   c. Vice areas catering primarily to whites must be contained within Negro areas and not allowed to exist within commercial and white residential areas.

2. Restrictions on occupational positions and on positions within organizations.[70]
   a. Negroes are not to be hired as long as a supply of white labor is available.
   b. Except in unions that have been organized in the major fields of Negro employment, Negroes are not to be admitted into unions. "At the turn of the century the AFL had fully capitulated to a policy of chauvinism and overt discrimination against Negroes, Orientals, and certain other ethnic groups."[71] The major techniques of discrimination utilized in both the North and the South were: "(1) exclusion from membership by racial provisions in union constitutions or ritual by-laws; (2) exclusion of Negroes by tacit agreement in the absence of written provisions; (3) segregated locals; (4) 'auxiliary' locals; (5) other forms of collusion; (6) separate racial seniority and promotional provisions in contracts, limiting Negro workers to menial or unskilled jobs; (7) control of licensing boards to exclude Negro workers from craft occupations; (8) refusal to

admit Negroes into union-controlled apprenticeship training programs;
(9) negotiating wages and other terms of employment affecting Negroes
while denying them admission into the collective bargaining unit; and
(10) denial of access to union hiring halls, where such hiring halls are the
exclusive source of labor supply."[72]

    c. Negro domestics are to receive less wages than white domestics for the
same work and are not to be placed in the position of head servant in a
large household.

    d. Negro professionals are to serve only other Negroes.

    e. White collar positions in the white dominated economy are to be restricted
to whites only. "The North is almost as strict as the South in excluding
Negroes from middle class jobs. . . ."[73]

3. Restrictions on business practices. Negro businessmen are poor credit risks
and loans to them are not advisable.[74]

4. Restrictions on municipal services and access to public buildings.[75]

    a. Negroes are to be excluded from white-owned commercial amusements—
such as skating rinks, dance halls, amusement parks, swimming pools.

    b. Negroes are to be segregated into the balcony of theatres.

    c. Only very prominent Negroes are to be served in restaurants. (Less
prominent Negroes were harassed or refused service.)

5. Restrictions on civil rights in terms of police action.[76]

    a. Negroes can be arrested on less pretext than can whites.

    b. Negroes do not have to be shown the same courtesy by the police as
whites, and Negroes may be arrested more vigorously than whites.

Major Differences between the North and the
South during the Period 1900-1940

The total system of constraints upon blacks in the North was considerably less
than in the South; however, in certain areas, there was very little difference:
residential discrimination; restrictions to lower status occupations; restrictions
on membership in unions; and discrimination in privately owned but public
facilities such as swimming pools, theatres, hotels, restaurants, and amusement
parks.

    Certain areas of discrimination were virtually lacking in Northern cities as
compared with the South. One of these areas was interpersonal restrictions or
"racial etiquette." Myrdal states, "The Northern pattern could hardly be called
an etiquette because it does not require that Negroes act in a special way toward
whites or that whites act in a special way toward Negroes. Rather it takes the
form of institutionalizing and rendering impersonal limited number of types of

segregation: Negroes are requested not to use bathing beaches reserved for whites; Negroes are requested not to patronize certain dance halls, hotels, and restaurants, and things are made unpleasant for them if they do."[77] In the North, discrimination on public carriers was virtually nonexistent.[78] In addition, little restrictions on voting were placed on blacks in the North. However, some Northern cities did practice gerrymandering of political districts which restricted the influence of the black vote.[79]

Relatively speaking, discrimination in several other areas was less in the North than the South. Police in the South enforced discrimination and *apartheid* as part of a moral order. In the North, outside of the occasional acts of prejudiced policemen, differential treatment by police was more on a class basis than of a racial one. Myrdal emphasizes that, ". . . on the whole, Negroes do not meet much more discrimination from officers of the law than do white persons of the same economic and cultural level. . . ."[80] Segregation in the public schools, although due in part to discrimination in the form of gerrymandering of school districts, was primarily the result of residential discrimination. There was little school segregation required by law in the North and West (Arizona required it in the elementary grades).[81] However, because of the indirect effects of residential segregation and discrimination, the North was almost as segregated as the South in terms of public schools.

A major issue, then, as now, is whether life in a black ghetto is due to the voluntary desire to maintain some way of life or whether this life style is a necessary and involuntary adaption to white discrimination. Spear examines this problem as it related to Chicago in the early twentieth century, and although his argument may not be applicable today with the increasing emphasis on black pride and the black community, it was probably true for American cities in this historical period.

The Chicago experience, therefore, tends to refute any attempt to compare Northern Negroes with European immigrants. Unlike the Irish, Poles, Jews, or Italians, Negroes banded together not to enjoy a common linguistic, cultural, and religious tradition, but because a systematic pattern of discrimination left them no alternative. Negroes were tied together less by a common cultural heritage than by a common set of grievances. . . . From its inception, the Negro ghetto was unique among the city's ethnic enclaves. It grew in response to an implacable white hostility that has not basically changed. In this sense it has been Chicago's only true ghetto, less the product of voluntary development within than of external pressures from without. . . . No physical wall has encircled the black belt. But an almost equally impervious wall of hostility and discrimination has isolated Negroes from the mainstream of Chicago life. Under such conditions, Negroes have tried, often against impossible odds, to make the best of their circumstances by creating a meaningful life of their own. But they have done so, not out of choice, but because white society has left them no alternative.[82]

3

Changes in Racial Discrimination and Racial Stratification Since World War II

Change in Social Stratification Systems

All social systems are formed or come into being, become structured or institutionalized, and eventually they are transformed into some new system of human relationships. A new social system may be said to exist when a new *configuration* of continuous and discontinuous (innovations) sociocultural elements are distinctively different from an earlier configuration. *When* this new system of human relationships is formed in time is subject to disagreement due to scholarly focus on sociocultural continuity *or* focus on sociocultural discontinuity. This social system change occurs whether the system in question is a civilization, a society, an institution, a community, or, of importance here—a social stratification system.

In the United States, a system of black-white racial stratification (slavery) came into being between the years 1660 and 1750; became stabilized, formalized and legitimated in the latter half of the eighteenth century and the first half of the nineteenth century; and was transformed through social conflict in the form of the Civil War and Reconstruction. *Apartheid,* a new racial system of stratification formed in the last two decades of the nineteenth century, was made up of many continuous sociocultural elements from the slave pattern (particularly racist ideological beliefs, restriction on black male and white female sexual relations, and the occupational restriction of black people to the lowest of menial positions); the discontinuous elements were the elimination of human beings as chattel property, the establishment of *apartheid* as the norm in race relations, and the development of a more competitive pattern of stratification.

It can be strongly argued that this second system which was institutionalized and stabilized during the period from 1915 to 1940, is now undergoing transformation since World War II. This new pattern that is beginning to emerge is not yet identifiable and can still take various forms—equalitarian social and cultural pluralism; assimilation; the formation of a separate black nation-state out of present United States territory; one based on an increasing class division between the haves and the have-nots where race loses its significance; or the highly improbable pattern of reversed stratification (blacks dominate whites).

But whatever the new pattern of social stratification in America will be, it will not be a return to discriminatory *apartheid* based upon the biological

33

doctrine of racism. Many social change factors have been stressed by various social scientists that have undermined this second, and once-stable social system of race relations. The following factors seem to be the most important:

Major Factors Producing Change in Racial Stratification since World War II

Employment opportunities created by the war. "With the entry of the United States into World War II, Negro workers for the first time took a giant step toward equality with whites. The drafting of hundreds of thousands of civilian workers into the Armed Services created an acute labor shortage, and the dearth of qualified white males led to the recruitment of white women and Negroes of both sexes into types of work that previously had been largely closed to them."[1] "With the return of veterans to the civilian labor force at the end of the war, with the end of the Fair Employment Practices Committee in 1946, and with the decline of industries that mainly served the war effort, Negroes suffered losses in occupational status. However, not all wartime gains were lost, and conditions remained more favorable for Negro advancement than they had been before the war. Negro servicemen and workers in war industries gained valuable training and experience that enabled them to compete more effectively, and their employment in large numbers in unionized industries during the war left them in a stronger position in the labor movement."[2]

Changes in the economy. "During and since the war, hundreds of thousands of new jobs have been created at intermediate and upper levels, and many Negroes have been able to move up without displacing whites. . . . Because Negro gains could occur without loss to whites, white resistance to Negro advancement was less than it otherwise would have been."[3] In addition, since by 1940 European immigration had declined to a trickle, there was no longer a large pool of white immigrants at the lowest occupational levels to replace the upward-moving white native workers.[4] The increased industrialization of the South has changed the structure of power among whites to groups not historically committed to the traditional patterns of race relations. Vander Zanden has noted that the ". . . control of the regional power structure has moved from the landed classes to the industrial and financial classes. Within the Deep South the balance of power is shifting from the rural Tidewater section to the industrial Piedmont. The reigns of control are changing from the hands of the region's old families to those of the new financiers and officials in the absentee-owned corporations."[5] With the rise of new industries, ". . . professionals and personnel for the new bureaucratic structures have come from the outside, many of them from the

North. These new leaders tend to dislodge the old families of local merchants and manufacturers from their dominant positions."[6]

Increasing urbanization of the black American. Before World War II, in the decade 1930-1940, the net outmigration from the South by blacks was 348,000. During the war and after, in the decade 1940-1950, this net outmigration rose rapidly to 1,597,000. Continued migration out of the South in the 1950s and 1960s has now reduced the proportion of all blacks living in the South to 55% (compared with 91% in 1910).[7] This northern migration was primarily to large metropolitan areas and today American blacks are more urbanized than whites (about 70% compared with 64% for whites in 1966).[8] In addition, many of the blacks that did not leave the South did leave rural areas and migrated to Southern cities. The number of rural Southern blacks declined from 5.4 million in 1950 to 4.8 million in 1960, so that in 1966 more than half of the Southern black population now lives in urban areas. Only in four Southern states—Arkansas, Mississippi, North Carolina, and South Carolina—do rural blacks outnumber urban blacks.[9]

The behavioral consequences of this migration are numerous. Of particular significance is the increasing transformation of a predominately black peasant class in the South to an urbanized proletariat class and the replacement of more powerful rural social controls by the more tenuous, formalized and secondary social controls of city life. Riots and rebellions by an urbanized black proletariat in ghettos of increasing density and deterioration were a major part of life in America in the 1960s. To many whites, the police are a "thin blue line" to protect suburban white America from black crime, protest, and black revolution.

The decline in the political power of Southern Democratic Party. ". . . no major political party can concede to Southern demands without seriously endangering its popularity outside of the South. The practical possibility that the Democratic Party can emerge as the effective voice for the South on the national scene no longer exists, as it did in the nineteenth century. Instead, its northern leaders champion civil rights programs. Since the 1930s two developments of importance have occurred. First, by the nature of its social and economic programs, the Democratic Party has increased its strength outside the South and thus has become less dependent upon southern electoral votes. Second, the party has carried on a campaign that in its effect wooed the votes of Negroes."[10] The growth of the Republican Party in the South, along with the increasing ability of blacks to engage in the political process, divides white politicians in competition over black votes (the very thing that occurred in the 1880s and 1890s which the formation of the "Solid South" eliminated).

The emergence of the United States as a world power since World War II. With the collapse of the traditional powers after World War II and the emergence of the U.S.S.R. and the United States as superpowers competing for dominance, a foreign policy on the part of the United States was necessary that would appeal to "the Third World." Such a policy would only be effective if the pattern of race relations in the United States was changed; hence, domestic race relations became a matter of concern at the national level.

Nationalism in Africa and Asia. The rapid growth of nationalism that occurred in Africa and Asia after World War II terminated white colonialism in many areas, undermined the ideas of "colored" inferiority, and presented a new image and a new potential for black Americans. "Negritude," "black pride," and a revival of interest in African heritage are powerful factors in affecting the black man's sense of identity and the elimination of the subservient and demeaning traditional black role.

Developments in social science which have undermined the doctrine of biological racism. "Since the 1920s, social science opinion in the United States has undergone a complete reversal from general acceptance to an almost unanimous rejection of the theory of innate racial inferiority of Negroes.... An examination of changing social science opinion concerning racial differences may explain both the reinforcement of racist ideas at one period and their elimination at another. This would, in addition, support Tumin's observations that there is a lag of about 20 years between basic findings in race-relations research and the beginning of their implementation by government and society. Current public attitudes on race reflect, in part, earlier opinions in the social sciences."[11] Biological racism was the major ideological legitimation of both the slave system and the apartheid system of racial stratification in America, and although many white Americans are still biological racists, recent studies seem to indicate that the majority of whites no longer accept biological inferiority of blacks.[12] According to Schuman, the majority of whites today explain black inequality with the idea that blacks lack ambition and motivation to change their circumstances.[13]

The increased development of black competitive ability and black power. The most important of these social change factors has been the increased organization, competitiveness, power, and protests of black Americans, themselves. Although such black organizations as the NAACP and the Urban League go back to the early twentieth century, their effectiveness was extremely limited until other changes weakened the once stable and highly unified white power structure. However, since the war, these and other organizations, along with black citizens generally, have been the major force in affecting changes in race relations (see Chapter 5). This development cannot be stressed too fully, since all of the previously cited changes would be relatively uninfluential if blacks did not demand changes in role relationships and the elimination of inequality and discrimination. Docile and submissive blacks accepting white dominance can conceivably exist in cities as well as rural areas, they can do undesirable jobs in factories as well as on farms, they can demonstrate voting apathy regardless of changes in political parties, and they can be so peaceful and happy that foreign policy is not endangered. But it is precisely the fact that they are *not* docile, submissive, apathetic, and overtly "happy" that the other changes have significance.

Antiracial discrimination public policies. Reacting to these changes (and "reaction" is the most suitable term) governmental bodies have issued decisions, passed laws, and formulated public policies which have further transformed this second system of racial stratification. Since public policy is a major part of the UNITAR guidelines, this change factor will be more extensively examined in the following section.

Public Policies Directed against Racial Discrimination since World War II

Governments, local or national, formulate and carry out policies to produce certain desired changes. These changes, whether a restoration of the *status quo* is intended or some modification of the present system is the goal, are, in either case, *functional*. Public policies are functional in the sense that the changes that are desired are intended to perpetuate the established system (whether this system is the traditional system or one recently established by revolution). The intent of policy is not to threaten the position or vested interests of the policy formulators. Obviously, some public policies do threaten or undermine the position of the policy formulators, but this is a latent or unintended consequence, not the manifest function.

If this is true (i.e., public policy is functional), then before *specific* policies directed against discrimination can be examined, a major question must be raised—is a racist society capable of instigating and enforcing policies designed to eliminate racial discrimination (admittedly, a loaded question)? Tilden J. LeMelle, in an unpublished paper presented to the International Research Conference on Race Relations at Aspen, Colorado, in 1970, made the following argument related to this question:

... one may seriously question whether a society such as that of the United States is really capable of legislating and enforcing effective public policy to combat racial discrimination. Perhaps the most effective function of such legislation might be simply providing an aura of legitimacy for more direct political action to combat racial discrimination—particularly political action by the victims of the racial discrimination. . . . Whether a society in which racism has been internalized and institutionalized to the point of being an essential and inherently functioning component of that society—a culture from whose inception racial discrimination has been a regulative force for maintaining stability and growth and for maximizing other cultural values—whether such a society *of itself* can even legislate (let alone enforce) public policy to combat racial discrimination is most doubtful. The history of man offers no evidence of any society consciously legislating itself out of existence. To the contrary, radical cultural changes have occurred only after the demise of those societies stubbornly adhering to old values and their institutional representations. . . . A racist culture—can move to eradicate or make racism ineffective only when racism itself becomes a serious threat to the culture and its bearers. United States society, therefore, can legislate and enforce public policy to combat racial discrimination only when continued racial discrimination begins to be more a serious threat to the existing American culture than the useful regulator it has been.[14]

This question, raised by LeMelle (and partially answered), cannot be answered in this preliminary examination of policy and discrimination. However, Chapter 5—dealing with an examination of the variables that affect the degree to which policy is effective—may provide some insight into the question: Can public policy make *any* impression on eliminating racial discrimination in a society that has traditionally been racist?

Four general types of public policies related to reducing and eliminating racial discrimination and racial inequality are identifiable. The first type is concerned with guaranteeing the civil rights of minority groups by eliminating the restrictions that have historically been placed as barriers to the freedom of action of these groups. What is generally assumed in this traditional civil rights policy is that elimination of illegitimate discrimination will have effect upon the inequality of the subordinant racial group.

The second type of policy may be termed "affirmative action" or "preferential treatment." This type of policy goes further than the first in that pressure is put upon the targets of the policy to take some form of positive action other than just eliminating the barriers to hire minorities, to integrate schools or neighborhoods, to promote minority business, to increase the level of education of minority races, etc. A major argument justifying this type of policy is that eliminating discriminatory barriers and restrictions, by itself, is insufficient *if* greater equality of the races is desired. As Coleman has stated, ". . . not long ago many persons held the simple assumption that elimination of the strictures of action directly due to skin color would somehow erase all the social deficits held by Negroes. Though the elimination of skin color constraints is far from realization, enough change has occurred, principally through legal action and legislation, to make quite clear that the other deficits will not be automatically erased, even if skin color comes to play no part in human interaction."[15] The reason for this is the effects of past discrimination. Some form of quotas may be used in the policy, such as establishing a population ratio distribution in occupational positions or union membership; however, quotas are not necessary to the policy. There is a feature of affirmative action policies that distinguishes this type from the third type in that affiliation with a group of victims is included as *one* of the relevant criteria given positive weight along with other criteria such as skill, educational background, etc.[16] In the third type of policy, racial affiliation is the sole criteria for preferential treatment.

The third type of policy, not yet (if ever) an aspect of American governmental action, may be called "discrimination-in-reverse." Discrimination-in-reverse is a policy whereby the allocation of resources, services, and opportunities are primarily based on group affiliation to the exclusion of or subordination of technically relevant criteria for determining such allocations.[17] Strictly by virtue of one's minority racial status, an individual is given preferential treatment over individuals of a majority racial status, regardless of qualification. Again, quotas may be used in this policy, but are not essential to this type. Given this distinction between affirmative action and discrimination-in-reverse, it should be clear that governmental policies stressing affirmative action are not reversed racism, nor is some desired quota goal necessarily discriminatory to a dominant race.

The last type of policy does not *directly* focus on racial issues or racial discrimination. This type is concerned with programs designed to reduce inequality generally, primarily focusing on the lowest socioeconomic strata. Essentially beginning with the New Deal in 1933 (but perhaps even earlier with the establishment of the graduated income tax under Woodrow Wilson) and continuing to the present in such policies as the "War on Poverty" and programs to increase housing to low income groups (Model Cities Program), the federal government has been committed to such a policy. Because of their disproportionate distribution in the lower income levels, blacks and American Indians should benefit, as groups, more than whites by such policies, although, in sheer *numbers of individuals*, whites are affected predominately. In any case, the effect on racial inequality is a latent function.

Since this book is concerned with policies directed against *racial discrimination* as its major focus, this complex area of economic and political change will not be examined, except to point out two specific subtypes of this policy which have often not been kept clear by governmental programs. These two specific types of policies designed to eliminate or diminish general inequality, according to Coleman, are permanent dependency and self-sufficiency. In the permanent dependency policy, a number of dependent households would be supported by public funds, either through direct payments or disguised by subsidized noncompetitive industries or public works. The second type would have as its goal a state in which all households in the society are independent of external support. This policy may involve such programs as increasing job opportunity through protected industries which are eventually liquidated as the occupational experience provides personal resources sufficient to make the households competitive, and the providing of services to help overcome deficits of the poor such as housing, educational programs, training programs, health services, child care centers, etc.[18] These subtypes are noted in this book dealing with race because of the fact that since blacks and Indians are disproportionately distributed in the lower strata, a policy of permanent dependency could very likely perpetuate the majority of two minority races in a position of permanent wards of the state with all of the racist consequences of such a status.

In the area of employment opportunity, governmental policy began in 1941 after a threatened march on Washington by A. Philip Randolph, President of the Brotherhood of Sleeping Car Porters, protesting discrimination in war industries; a federal fair employment practices law with a federal commision was enacted as the result of this action. This commission was disbanded after the war in 1946. Subsequently, following the lead of New York State in 1945, the majority of states have established state fair employment practices commissions. Under President Kennedy, Executive Order 10925 was issued in 1962 which established an Equal Employment Opportunities Commission which was empowered to withhold federal contracts with private companies unless the contractor undertakes "affirmative action to ensure that applicants are employed, and that employees are treated during employment, without regard to their race, creed, color or national origin." Under Title VII of the 1964 Civil Rights Act, an Equal Employment Opportunities Commission was established which superceded the earlier commission. This commission is empowered to handle individual complaints of discrimination in private companies engaging in interstate commerce with employment of 25 or more regular employees, in labor unions if they operate a hiring hall for covered employers, or if they have 25 or more members employed by a covered employer. In addition, employment agencies are covered by the act if they regularly undertake to supply employees for a covered employer. Notably absent from Title VII are employees of federal, state, and local government, private clubs, educational and religious institutions. The commission may investigate the complaint, and if valid, utilize persuasion and conciliation with the company or union. If such efforts fail after 60 days, the individual who brought the complaint may take his case to a federal court.[19] On September 24, 1965, President Johnson issued Executive Order 11246. This order establishes the Office of Federal Contract Compliance (OFCC) to be housed in the Department of Labor and supercedes all previous executive orders. The OFCC is a supervisory and coordinating agency charged with guaranteeing nondiscrimination in corporations and businesses that have a contract with the federal government. It supervises and coordinates fifteen "contracting agencies" of the federal government. The largest of these contracting agencies is the Department of Defense which has responsibility for 75% of all governmental contracts. The other fourteen agencies are the Department of Health, Education and Welfare, the Department of Housing and Urban Development, the Department of Transportation, the Department of Commerce, the Department of Agriculture, the Treasury Department, the National Aeronautics and Space Administration, the Post Office, the Department of the Interior, the Agency for Internal Development, the Tennessee Valley Authority, the Veterans Administration, the General Services Administration, and the Atomic Energy Commission. It is estimated that one-third of the nation's total labor force is employed by federal governmental contractors and more than 100,000 contractor facilities are covered by this Executive Order 11246.[20]

Fair housing policies by government first began in New York City in 1939 and then spread to other cities and states. As of December 1967, 88 local housing laws had been passed and 21 states had fair housing laws; at this date, an estimated 118 million people, or some 60% of the population lived under some form of local or state housing laws.[21] These state and local laws primarily only cover discrimination in multiple housing accommodations that are privately owned and discrimination in public and publicly assisted housing. These laws are typically administered by a board or commission made up of appointed citizens with a small professional staff. Their methods of compliance vary—some can only investigate on the basis of a complaint and then use persuasion and conciliation, others can instigate their own investigations and issue cease and desist orders which are enforced by the courts.[22]

The major court cases that have ruled against racial discrimination in housing have been *Shelley* v. *Kraemer* in 1948, which held that restrictive covenants were nonenforceable in the courts, and *Jones* v. *Mayer Co.* in 1968, in which the Supreme Court of the United States held that a 1866 law, passed under the authority of the Thirteenth Amendment, bars *all* racial discrimination, private as well as public, in the sale or rental of property.

Prior to the *Shelley* decision, the Federal Housing Administration (FHA) supported the practice of restrictive covenants and racially homogeneous neighborhoods. After *Shelley*, in late 1949, the FHA ruled that it would not provide mortgage insurance with respect to properties on which restrictive covenants were recorded after February 15, 1950.[23] In 1960, the FHA ruled that it *could* stop business with real estate brokers who discriminated in selling and renting acquired property.[24] On November 20, 1962, President Kennedy issued an executive order barring discrimination in all housing that received federal aid after that date.[25] In 1968, another Civil Rights Act was passed. Title VIII of this act states: "It is the policy of the United States to provide, within constitutional limitations, for fair housing throughout the United States."[a] Principle responsibility for administration and enforcement of this section lies with the Office of Housing Opportunity in HUD; this agency has no authority to issue cease and desist orders nor can it institute litigation. It can only use informal methods of conference, conciliation and persuasion, and if state and local housing laws exist that are "substantially equivalent," then HUD is required to refer complaints to their agencies.[26]

Antidiscrimination in public schools began with the Supreme Court decision in *Brown* v. *Board of Education* in 1954 in which the "separate but equal" doctrine of *Plessy* v. *Ferguson* in 1896 was reversed. Segregated schools were declared unconstitutional. In a subsequent decision in June 1955, the Supreme Court ruled that school authorities have a duty to initiate desegregation and bring about a constitutional operation of their school systems and lower courts were admonished to judge whether or not the action of school boards constitutes "good faith implementation of the governing constitutional principles."[27] Between 1954 and 1964, what little integration that took place in the South (the applicability of *Brown* to *de facto* segregation in the North was not clear) was accomplished by the National Association for the Advancement of Colored People bringing suits against school boards through the courts and not by any national administrative action. After the passing of the Civil Rights Act of 1964, following the Birmingham incident and the assassination of President Kennedy, the Office of Education in the Department of Health, Education and Welfare was directed by Title VI of this act to withhold federal funds from schools (and considerable federal money was available after the passage of the 1965 Elementary and Secondary Education Act). Upon what basis the federal money was to be withheld led to the development of the first guidelines. These guidelines, officially issued in April 1965, were essentially related to the idea of "freedom of choice." To receive federal money, school districts had to submit desegregation plans in which students were offered a choice before entrance to school, and any effort to make this process complicated or embarrassing for black students would not be tolerated. The third major step in discrimination in education policy (the first being judicial enforcement between 1954-1964 and the second being the HEW administrative use of Title VI based on "freedom of choice") was the development of a second set of guidelines by HEW in 1965

---

[a]This act now applies to virtually everybody with the exception of people who sell their house without using real estate offices, real estate salesmen, and who do not advertise in the paper.

which demanded *integration* based upon affirmative action to abolish separate schools and separate faculties. These second guidelines were supported by a decision in the 5th Circuit Court of Appeals (*U.S.* v. *Jefferson County Board of Education*) in December 1966 and by the U.S. Supreme Court in May, 1968 (*U.S.* v. *New Kent County Board of Education*).[28] On July 3, 1969, the fourth phase in a changing and often confusing policy was issued by the Attorney General and the Secretary of HEW. These third guidelines stated: (1) desegregation will be mainly through litigation brought by the Department of Justice, and HEW's administrative use of threat of termination of federal funds will be deemphasized; (2) the two departments will begin a program of desegregation in the regions other than the South where *de facto* school segregation exists; (3) the departments will refuse to require the completion of desegregation by any particular date or by means of a single arbitrary system; and (4) freedom of choice plans are acceptable.[29] As is apparent, with the exception of policy directed against the Northern and Western regions, federal policy as of 1969 has reverted back to the second phase of 1965, and with its emphasis on judicial litigation to the ineffective first phase.

Discrimination in voting has essentially become a matter of federal governmental policy since the passing of the Voting Rights Act of 1965. This act, directed against the states in the Deep South, provides for federal examiners to ensure nondiscrimination in voting, empowers the Department of Justice to bring suit to offenders, and provides a fine of not more than $5,000 or imprisonment for not more than five years as punishment for guilty offenders. The Civil Rights Act of 1968 provides criminal penalties for intimidation of persons engaging in voting, qualifying for voting, campaigning for public office, or poll watching. This 1968 amendment does not include, however, intimidation directed against campaign *workers*.[30]

Antiracial discrimination in public accommodations has been governmental policy in many Northern states since the nineteenth century; however, federal governmental policy primarily directed against the South is contained in Title II of the Civil Rights Act of 1964. Discrimination on the basis of race, color, religion, or national origin is forbidden in hotels and motels, restaurants, lunch counters, movie houses, gasoline stations, theatres, and stadiums. In addition, discrimination is forbidden in any other place or public accommodation that is required to segregate by state or local laws. If there are no segregation laws, Title II does not cover service establishments such as barbershops and beauty parlors (except in hotels), retail stores that do not serve food, and private clubs. Enforcement is in the form of judicial litigation initiated by individuals or by the Attorney General of the U.S.[31]

The final area that has been a major concern of governmental antidiscrimination policy is segregation in the armed forces. On July 28, 1948, President

Truman issued an executive order abolishing racial segregation in all of the armed forces of the United States. A committee was established to implement this order, with the Korean War hastening the carrying out of this policy.[32]

In summary, nine significant and major social changes have occurred, essentially beginning during World War II, which have begun to affect a once-stable system of racial stratification. Without any effort to ascertain the relative significance of each of these nine factors, what has been the extent of change, if any, in patterns of racial discrimination and racial inequality? Although the evidence is often incomplete, the following conclusions can be tentatively proposed in particular areas.

The Extent of Change in Racial Discrimination and Racial Inequality in Selected Areas

Occupation and Income

1) The ratio of nonwhite to white median family income has changed little since World War II; nonwhite being approximately one-half that of white (see Table 3-1).[33]

Table 3-1

Median Family Income, 1947-1968

Selected Years	White	Nonwhite*	Ratio of Nonwhite to White
1947	$3,157	$1,614	57
1949	3,232	1,650	51
1950	3,445	1,869	54
1955	4,605	2,549	55
1960	5,835	3,233	55
1965	7,251	3,886	54
1966	7,792	4,506	58
1967	8,274	4,919	59
1968	8,937	5,360	60

*From 1947 to 1960 in this table, "nonwhite" is utilized; from 1965 to 1968, "Negro" is used. Although not strictly comparable, blacks make up 92% of the nonwhite category; in addition, the higher incomes of Japanese and Chinese-Americans would not favorably affect the nonwhite figures since the lower incomes of American Indians would counteract this.

Source: U.S. Department of Labor, Bureau of Labor Statistics, *The Negro in the United States: Their Economic and Social Situation*, Bulletin No. 1511 (1966), Table III A-1, p. 138. U.S. Department of Commerce, "Selected Characteristics of Persons and Families," *Population Characteristics*, Bureau of Census Series P-20, No. 189, August 8, 1969, p. 4.

2) Blacks have made significant gains in the intermediate occupations (such as clerical workers, craftsmen, foreman, and operatives) between 1940 and 1960,[b] but there has been only a negligible increase in the higher-level occupations.[34] In government employment, during the first four years of the Equal Employment Program, blacks have garnered 20% of the new positions in federal service, with a virtual doubling of black occupancy of positions at the GS 12-18 level; however, blacks are still only 1% of those in GS 12-18, and 2.9% of those positions at the GS 9-11 levels.[36] Specifically, at the higher levels of government employment as of 1967, there was one black out of 125 top positions in the Executive Office of the President; of the forty-four largest federal independent agencies, there are 183 commissioners, members of the board, executive directors, and administrators, and seven of these were black; of the 220 assistant secretaries and deputy assistant secretaries in the twelve Cabinet departments of the Army, Navy, and Air Force, there were five blacks represented (and these were in four departments—HEW, Labor, State, and Agriculture); there were *no* blacks in any policy-making or responsible administrative positions in 103 departments of the federal government (such as Bureau of Prisons, Coast Guard, Commodity Credit Corporation, Forest Service, Rural Electrification Administration, Patent Office, Food and Drug Administration, etc.).[37]

At the level of managers, officials and professionals in the largest corporations, a recent survey of 441 of such corporations found that while blacks accounted for 7.9% of the employees, they only accounted for .9% of the managers and officials and 1.2% of the professional staff.[38] In a study of a single county, Cook County, Illinois, in 1965, 10,997 policy-making positions in all sectors were identified; blacks, while they were 20% of the population, only occupied 285 of these positions, or 2.6%. In 6838 policy-making positions in business corporations, blacks occupied 42 of these positions, or .6%.[39]

At the rate of change in occupational distribution by race between 1960 and 1968, Norvall Glenn has calculated a projection into the future in terms of what years particular occupational categories will have proportional racial distribution. Blacks will not attain professional and technical proportional representation until the year 2001, managerial and official proportional representation until 2083, clerical in the year 1981, sales by 2048, and in the category of craftsmen, foreman, and kindred occupations, proportional representation in the year 1995.[40]

3) Blacks have made substantial progress toward proportional representation by position and vocation in the Armed Forces, particularly the Army and the Air Force; however, at the highest levels, the change in proportional representation has been minimal.

---

[b] 1970 Census data not available at the time of this writing.

Table 3-2

Ratio of Actual to Expected Proportion of Employed Black Workers, in Each Occupational Group, United States, 1940, 1950, 1960*

Occupational Group	Male			Female		
	1940	1950	1960	1940	1950	1960
Professional, technical, and kindred workers	.33	.29	.30	.33	.45	.55
Farmers and farm managers	1.44	1.28	.77	2.20	2.24	1.06
Managers, proprietors, and officials, except farm	.13	.19	.17	.19	.30	.28
Clerical and kindred workers	.19	.47	.70	.04	.14	.25
Sales workers	.13	.17	.19	.07	.16	.19
Craftsmen, foreman, and kindred workers	.30	.42	.50	.16	.41	.54
Private household workers	7.00	5.71	5.32	3.38	4.87	4.60
Service workers, except private household	1.92	2.27	2.32	.92	1.55	1.58
Farm laborers and foremen	2.44	2.14	2.55	4.49	2.61	2.47
Laborers, except farm and mine	2.44	2.92	2.96	.96	1.88	1.85

*The expected proportion of blacks in each occupational group is the proportion of blacks in the total employed labor force. For instance, 8.4 percent of all employed males in 1960 were black, and one might "expect" 8.4 percent of employed males in each occupational group to be black, if there were no racial stratification. If the actual proportion of blacks in an occupational group is more than this parity, the ratio is greater than 1.00; if the actual proportion was less than expected, the ratio is less than 1.00.
Source: Adapted with permission of the publisher from Leonard Broom and Norval D. Glenn, *Transformation of the Negroe American* (New York: Harper & Row, 1965), p. 10.

Prior to World War II, about 6% of the Army consisted of segregated black units assigned primarily to noncombatant tasks, the Navy allowed blacks to join only as stewards in the messman's branch, and there were no black Marines before the War. During the war, blacks in the Army were utilized essentially as noncombatants, with the exception of the Ardennes battle during the winter of 1944-45; the Navy opened up a few positions for blacks,

Table 3-3[35]

Percentage Distribution of White and Black Labor Force by Occupational Field

| | 1940 | | 1950 | | 1960 | |
	White	Black	White	Black	White	Black
All sectors	100.0	100.0	100.0	100.0	100.0	100.0
Nonfarm, total	82.3	66.6	81.6	79.5	92.7	88.7
White collar total	35.7	6.0	39.9	10.2	46.5	15.4
Professional & technical	8.0	2.7	8.6	3.4	12.2	4.7
Proprietors, Managers and Officials	9.0	1.3	9.8	2.0	11.5	2.3
Clerical and Sales	18.7	2.0	21.5	4.8	22.8	8.4
Manual and service total	46.6	60.6	47.7	69.3	46.2	73.3
Skilled workers & foreman	12.2	3.0	14.4	5.5	13.8	5.7
Semiskilled & operatives	19.0	10.3	20.3	18.3	17.8	20.7
Laborers	6.1	14.3	5.0	15.7	4.4	14.1
Service workers	9.3	33.0	8.0	29.8	10.2	32.8
Farm, total	16.7	32.8	11.1	19.0	7.3	11.3

Source: Adapted with permission of the publisher from Dale L. Hiestand, *Economic Growth and Employment Opportunities for Minorities* (New York: Columbia University Press, 1964), p. 42.

primarily noncombatant tasks at segregated harbor and shore assignments; and the Marine Corps, in 1942, accepted blacks into the service where they were assigned to segregated units as ammunition handlers, heavy-duty laborers, and antiaircraft gunners.[41] Since World War II, considerable progress has been made at lower levels. In 1964, the percentage of blacks of the total personnel was 12.3 in the Army, 8.6 in the Air Force, 5.1 in the Navy, and 8.2 in the Marine Corps.[42] Utilizing these figures for the respective services, if racial proportional representation existed then, these percentages should exist at each level (see Table 3-4). The ratio of black to white officers is roughly 1 to 30 in the Army, 1 to 70 in the Air Force, 1 to 250 in the Marine Corps, and 1 to 300 in the Navy; blacks are underrepresented in the top three enlisted ranks in the Army and the top four ranks in the other three services.[43] Nevertheless, this situation when compared to pre-World II (when there were only five black officers in the entire armed forces, of which three were chaplains) represents extensive social change. The existence of less racial discrimination in the armed forces as compared with the civilian economy is

Table 3-4

Blacks as a Percentage of Total Personnel in Each Grade for Each Service, 1964

Grade	Army	Air Force	Navy	Marine Corps
Expected black percentage if proportional	12.3	8.6	5.1	8.2
Officers, actual percentage	3.4	1.5	0.3	0.4
Generals/Admirals	0.0	0.2	0.0	0.0
Colonels/Captains	0.2	0.2	0.0	0.0
Lt. Colonels/Commanders	1.1	0.5	0.6	0.0
Majors/Lt. Commanders	3.6	0.8	0.3	0.3
Captains/Lieutenants	5.4	2.0	0.5	0.4
1st. Lieutenants/Lts. j.g.	3.8	1.8	0.2	0.4
2nd. Lieutenants/Ensigns	2.7	2.5	0.7	0.3
Enlisted, actual percentage	13.4	10.0	5.8	8.7
E-9 (Sgt. Major)	3.5	1.2	1.5	0.8
E-8 (Master Sgt.)	6.1	2.2	1.9	1.2
E-7 (Sgt. 1st class)	8.5	3.2	2.9	2.3
E-6 (Staff Sgt.)	13.9	5.3	4.7	5.0
E-5 (Sgt.)	17.4	10.8	6.6	11.2
E-4 (Corporal)	14.2	12.7	5.9	10.4
E-3 (Pvt. 1st class)	13.6	9.7	6.6	7.8
E-2 (Private)	13.1	11.7	5.7	9.5
E-1 (Recruit)	6.8	14.4	7.1	9.1

Source: Adapted with permission of the publisher from Charles C. Moskos, "Racial Integration in the Armed Forces," *American Journal of Sociology* 72 (September 1966), 136-137.

illustrated when occupational levels within the services are compared with civilian jobs of comparable standing. "Negro enlisted men enjoy relatively better opportunities in the Armed Forces than in the civilian economy in every clerical, technical, and skilled field for which the data permit comparison."[44] Officers "... represent a larger proportion than Negro civilians in a number of fields which have been traditionally closed to them by historical patterns of discrimination. These include engineering, the applied sciences, finance and accounting, aviation, navigation, and a wide variety of management fields."[45]

4) Since 1955, segregation in labor unions has declined drastically, and formal

and overt racial discrimination has virtually been eliminated; however, informal and covert techniques still exist in many unions, and there has been little change in the building trades unions, with only token black representation.

In 1955, the CIO and the AFL merged, and this convention adopted resolutions to eliminate segregation and discrimination in the unions. In 1963, the last AFL-CIO affiliate removed the formalized barrier to black membership as found in discriminatory constitutions and rituals.[46] In this same year, of the 55,000 union locals in the AFL-CIO, only 172 in 19 affiliates were segregated.[47] But racial discrimination still exists in the form of a change from reliance upon formal and overt techniques to informal and covert methods to maintain the same discriminatory norms of earlier periods. These informal methods are several: informal agreements not to sponsor blacks for membership; ignoring the application of blacks into apprentice programs; refusal of journeyman status by means of examinations which are rigged so that blacks cannot pass them; exertion of political pressure on governmental licensing agencies to ensure that blacks fail the tests; restriction of membership to sons or relatives of the present members.[48]

Although these practices may be found among many locals, the major offenders are the building trades unions. Herbert Hill has stated the consequence of this continued discrimination: "Today, in virtually every large urban center in the United States, Negro workers are denied employment in the major industrial and residential construction projects because they are, with some few exceptions, barred from membership in the building trades craft unions."[49] Investigations by the NAACP and the U.S. Civil Rights Commission in various cities illustrate the token representation of blacks in these unions. As one example, the investigation in Cleveland in April 1966, revealed the following: The International Brotherhood of Electrical Workers, Local 38, with a total membership of 1258 had two black workers; Iron Workers, Local 17, with a membership of 1482 had three blacks; the Pipefitters Local 36 had one black member out of 1319; and the Sheet Metal Workers, Local 65, less discriminatory than most, had 45 black members out of a total membership of 1077.[50] Hill pessimistically concluded, "At the end of a decade of mass demonstrations, the filing of complaints with FEPC agencies, and the repeated attempts to secure enforcement of federal anti-discrimination executive orders, the five craft locals had four Negro apprentices."[51]

5) There has been only minimal change of black representation in law enforcement agencies, with only token representation, at best, in the South.

A study by the U.S. Commission on Civil Rights in 1963 found that few blacks were employed in northern and western police departments relative to their total population and in the South and the border states their representation was only token. In the state police and highway patrols, there was only one patrolman in twelve southern states and 33 black patrolmen in nineteen northern and western states. In 289 counties in the South and in the border states, there were only seven black lawyers, three investigators, and two stenographers in the county prosecutors' offices. In the state courts in the South, there were no black judges or court clerks, and 3% of the positions of jury commissioners, baliffs, and secretaries were occupied by blacks. One-thirtieth of the administrative, professional or clerical positions in state adult correctional institutions outside of the South were occupied by blacks; no black representation existed in Arkansas, Alabama, Georgia, Kentucky, Louisiana, Mississippi, Oklahoma, or Tennessee.[52] A study of racial representation of judges in New York City and in Chicago in 1967 found 17 black judges in the various city, state, and federal courts located in New York City out of 372 or 4.5% (blacks in New York City were estimated to be 21% of the population in 1967). In Chicago, where blacks are 31% of the population, there were 9 black judges out of a total of 152 or a percentage of 5.9%.[53]

Public Schools

1) Racial integration or desegregation of public schools in the South between the end of World War II and 1964 has been negligible with a slight increase since 1964; in the nation as a whole school segregation is increasing.

In 1964, after a decade of effort following the *Brown* decision, only Texas and Tennessee had more than 2% of their black students in integrated schools, and for the South as a whole, 1% of black students attended integrated schools.[54] Correlated with a policy change by the federal government in 1964 (use of Title VI of the 1964 Civil Rights Act by HEW), some change has occurred. In the 1968-69 school year, 15.1% of all black students attended desegregated schools in the Deep South, ranging from 7.1% in Mississippi to 27.8% in North Carolina.[55] Helping the "credibility gap," the Attorney General and the Secretary of HEW on July 3, 1969, announced that of the 4,477 school districts in 17 southern and border states 2,994 had desegregated voluntarily and completely. The Civil Rights Commission investigated this claim and found that at least 1,018 of these "completely desegregated" districts had no black students whatsoever.[56]

In the North, school segregation in urban schools is increasing. The U.S. Civil Rights Commission, in a sample of 15 large Northern cities, found that segregation had increased sharply from 1950 to 1965 with increases in black enrollment being absorbed by already predominately black schools—84% of increase being absorbed by schools more than 90% blacks.[57]

In the nation as a whole, then, no progress has been made in school integration. In fact, school segregation is greater than before World War II, and by 1975, it is estimated that if current policies and trends persist, 80% of all black pupils in the twenty largest cities, comprising nearly one-half of the nation's black population, will be attending 90 to 100% black schools.[58]

2) The number of years of schooling completed by blacks almost doubled since 1940, and the ratio of nonwhite years of schooling to white has been reduced.

The median number of years of school completed by blacks in 1940 was 5.8. By 1967, the median number of years completed had increased to 9.4. Although white levels of years-completed rose also, the ratio of the nonwhite to the white median years-completed increased from .67 in 1940 to .78 in 1967; if the 1960-67 rate of change continues this nonwhite-white ratio will be .80 in 1970 and 1.00 (equal) in the year 2010.[59] In terms of relative *quality* of black education to white, Glenn states, "There are no data that allow an accurate tracing of recent trends in the quality gap between Negro and white education, but there is little reason to believe the gap has diminished much during the 1960s."[60]

3) School desegregation in the South has meant the loss of status or of unemployment for many black educators, and segregation of faculties and of students within "integrated" schools has developed.

The National Education Association has estimated that at least 5,000 black principals and teachers have been subjected to wholesale demotion or dismissal throughout much of the South since desegregation began in 1954.[61] A report by six private civil rights groups issued November 24, 1970, stated that monitors of these organizations had found 94 cases of segregation within schools' classrooms or other facilities, 62 cases of faculty segregation, 47 cases of segregation in busing, and 98 cases of discrimination in dismissing or demoting black teachers or principals.[62] Besides assigning a black educator to inferior academic, or even nonacademic positions, which is overt discrimination, a common covert technique is to assign a black teacher to a subject in which he has no certification, closely observe him, then fire him for incompetence.[63] As specific examples, Fred McCoy, former principal of all-black Midway Elementary School in Natalbany, Louisiana, was assigned as a teacher in the morning and a latrine janitor in the afternoon after integration closed his school. James Noah, head coach of C.M. Washington High School in Thibodaux, Louisiana, became an assistant coach on the B team in his new integrated school. Wisdom Coleman, principal of a high school in Greenwood, Mississippi, became a hall monitor under Southern integration procedures.[64]

Housing and Residence

1) Residential segregation by race has remained virtually the same since 1940.

The Taeubers' studies of racial segregation in the largest American cities found an average segregation index[c] of 85.2 in 1940, 87.3 in 1950, and 86.2 in 1960 (in 1960 this index by regions was 79.3 in the West, 90.9 in the South, 79.2 in the Northeast, and 87.7 in the North Central states).[65] Since the war, black ghettos in the central cities have expanded in size and density, gradually enveloping previously all-white areas. As this "invasion-succession" has taken place, whites have moved to the suburbs, keeping the segregation index about the same. Between 1950 and 1966, 77.8% of the white population increase of 35.6 million people took place in the suburbs while the central cities received only 2.5% of this total white increase. The proportion of blacks within central cities has increased from 12% in 1950 to 20% in 1966, and metropolitan areas outside of the central cities remained 95% white from 1956 to 1960 and became 96% white in 1966.[66] Recent trends based upon preliminary examination of the 1970 census data indicate that blacks have begun to move to the suburbs, and the increase in the black population in the central cities as compared with the inner suburbs has declined.[67] Whether this indicates some integration of the suburbs or merely black expansion into inner suburbs already considered undesirable by whites who are leaving (i.e., more invasion-succession) will have to wait for further analysis.

2) Real estate discrimination since World War II has changed from overt and direct techniques to covert and indirect techniques which are equal to or superior to those of prewar discrimination.

Although the techniques have changed, the discriminatory norm remains the same—blacks are not to move into or reside in neighborhoods and areas desired by whites. The change in discriminatory techniques dates to the *Shelley* v. *Kraemer* Supreme Court decision in 1948. Denton aptly summarizes this change—"Prior to that decision the force exerted against

[c]The segregation index is based on the extent of racial residential segregation in city blocks. If blacks and whites are proportionately distributed according to the overall population within a city block, the index is 0. If a city block contains all whites or all blacks, the index is 100.

minorities was open and disguised; since then it has become covert and hypocritical. Some forms of organized racial discrimination have disappeared, but the *most effective* ones prevail, and new subtle forms beyond the reach of existing law have been developed."[68] Some of the major techniques now utilized by real estate specialists and city governments are: (1) use of zoning regulations—such as requiring a minimum lot size and minimum house size which prevents low income housing, limiting public housing to slum areas and prohibiting public housing in scattered and vacant areas;[69] (2) raising taxes or diminishing services in open housing areas; for example, in San Francisco, an open occupancy housing division had a sixfold increase in the cost of sewage connections, and in Dearborn, Michigan, a black moved into a white neighborhood and did not receive garbage collection and had his gas turned off;[70] (3) preventing black realtors from joining the National Association of Real Estate Boards on the grounds of vague generalizations about lack of experience, ability, or character;[71] (4) the use of membership clubs to which one must belong before being permitted to purchase real estate in a designated area;[72] (5) buy-back agreements which require owners offering their property for sale to give their neighbors, subdividers, or a neighborhood association first choice;[73] (6) unwillingness of white realtors to show blacks property in white areas;[74] (7) refusal of loans by mortgage loan officers to blacks buying property in white areas because the black buyer is not "qualified." Denton puts the major blame on real estate professionals. "There is ample evidence that both before the *Shelley* case and since, the dominant force in creating and maintaining ghettos is the activity of professionals in the real estate industry. This covers the whole spectrum of specialists such as appraisers, property managers, and mortage loan officers as well as home builders, escrow and title company officers, most of which are members of real estate boards affiliated with the NAREB."[75] Helper reaffirms this contention regarding brokers in her study of real estate brokers. She found that the unwillingness to sell or to rent property to blacks in a white area was the chief point of agreement among brokers based upon similar ideological beliefs—such as selling to blacks will lower property values, will affect their business, will lower their image, and that the cultural level of blacks is still far below whites.[76]

That discrimination is the major factor in creating residential segregation has been emphasized by Taeuber. He asks the question—what causes segregated housing; is it the result of poverty, of free choice, or discrimination? On the basis of his studies, he concludes, "A summary assessment can now be made of the three factors. Neither free choice nor poverty is a sufficient explanation for the universally high degree of segregation in American cities. Discrimination is the principle cause of Negro residential segregation, and there is no basis for anticipating major changes in the segregated character of American cities until patterns of housing discrimination can be altered."[77]

Political Participation

1) Black voting registration has increased significantly since 1940, although it is not yet proportionately equal to that of whites.

Table 3-5

Voting Registration in Eight Southern States, 1964, 1966, 1968

State	Percent of Voting Age Blacks Registered			Percent of Voting Age Whites Registered		
	1964	1966	1968	1964	1966	1968
Alabama	23.0	51.2	56.3	70.7	88.1	82.7
Arkansas	54.4	59.7	62.8	71.7	70.3	72.4
Florida	63.7	60.9	62.3	84.0	80.0	83.8
Georgia	44.0	47.2	54.5	74.5	76.7	80.6
Louisiana	32.0	47.1	58.5	80.4	83.1	87.0
Mississippi	6.7	32.9	62.5	70.1	62.9	88.9
South Carolina	38.8	51.4	49.3	78.5	80.2	63.6
Texas	57.7	61.6	83.1	53.2	53.3	72.3
Total	40.0	51.5	60.8	72.9	74.3	78.9

Source: Voting Education Project of the Southern Regional Council.

In 1940, a seven volume unpublished study by Dr. Ralphe Bunche entitled *The Political Status of the Negro*, estimated that between 80,000 and 90,000 blacks voted in that year's election in eight states in the South—Alabama, Arkansas, Florida, Georgia, Louisiana, Mississippi, South Carolina, and Texas. Stone, in his book *Black Political Power in America*, estimates that if 90,000 blacks voted and that 50% of all of those blacks that were registered voted, then black voting registration was 4% of "eligible" black voters.[78] If 4% of eligible blacks were registered in 1940, then the following table illustrates the sizable increase in voting registration in the same eight southern states: 40% in 1964 (before Voting Rights Act of 1965), 51.5% in 1966, and 60.8% in 1968.[79]

2) Although some forms of overt and direct political discrimination exist in the South, new forms of covert and indirect discriminatory techniques have been

developed, but these are not as effective in preventing black political participation as earlier methods were.

Some of the major discriminatory techniques now being utilized in various states and districts in the South are: switching to at-large elections where black voting strength is concentrated; redrawing lines of legislative districts to divide concentrations of black voting strength; initiating full-slate voting requirements (a voter must vote for somebody for all positions that are vacant on the slate or his ballot is disallowed; hence if 20 candidates are running for 10 positions in an at-large election, a black voter must vote for ten men, of which, say, only two may be black); abolishing offices sought by black candidates or making the office subject to appointment; extending the term of office of white incumbents; raising the filing fees of black candidates; omitting names of registered black voters from the voting list; increasing requirements to get on the ballot; withholding certification of the nominating petitions of black candidates until too late; failing to provide adequate voting facilities (e.g., too few voting machines for black areas produce discouraging long lines); disqualifying ballots of blacks on technical grounds; failure to provide assistance to illiterate black voters; withholding information about party precinct meetings; not giving blacks the same opportunity as whites to cast absentee ballots; making the endorsement of racial segregation a condition for running for office (Mississippi); selecting only white election officials or token blacks acceptable to whites; and establishing polling places in plantation stores where black farmers have credit (which may be harder to get if they vote).[80] The discriminatory norms—blacks shall not vote and blacks shall not run for public office—are still part of a 300 year-old Southern tradition; only the techniques of implementing these norms have changed.

3) There has been a slight increase in the number of black state and federal legislators with black legislative representation still far from proportional.

Between 1881 and 1966, there were no black federal Senators. Between 1901 and the beginning of World War II, there were two black Congressmen—Oscar S. De Priest (1929-1935) from Chicago and Arthur W. Mitchell (1935-1943), also from Chicago.[81] As of January 1969, the 91st Congress has nine black Congressmen and one Senator.[82] Hence, the 30-year period from 1940 to 1970 has seen the negligible increase of black national legislators from one to ten.

At the level of state legislators, the number of black representatives in 1940 could not be ascertained by this researcher; however, it is highly probable that the number of black representatives was negligible. As of November 1967, black legislators were found in 30 states. Within these 30 states, 126 out of 3281 members of the lower houses were black or 3.8%, and 31 out of 657 members of the state senates were black or 4.4%.[83]

These have been the major social changes, and lack of change, from the pre-World War II pattern of racial stratification. Although in the more personal areas of interaction, such as residence and schools, there has been virtually little change, some progress has been made in diminishing racial inequality and racial discrimination. From everything we know about social change and revolution, this slight overall progress has had, and will continue to have, a major influence on increasing social conflict between the races. Protests, conflict, and rebellion rarely take place when a subordinant group is severely dominated and unequal. These processes take place when a group is on the upswing, when some changes have been made and the possibility of greater changes can be anticipated. As Glenn and Bojean have stated, ". . . a temporary increase in conflict, violence, and social separation of the races may be an inevitable concomitant of an acceleration in some kinds of black progress."[84]

4 Major Independent Variables Affecting Policy Effectiveness

Public policies directed against racial discrimination vary as to effectiveness. If "effectiveness," the *dependent* variable, is defined as the degree to which policy goals are achieved,[1] then what are the major *independent* variables that affect the degree of goal achievement? A cursory examination of criticisms and evaluations of public policy, generally, and racial discrimination policies, in particular, indicate five very *general* variables: internal organizational efficiency, research, enforcement, support and resistance, and the comprehensiveness of the policy. The first variable relates to administrative factors *within* the organizations that implement policy, while the other four are concerned with the interaction of policy organizations with the environment they are attempting to change. If the organizations that implement policy are internally efficient, if knowledge based upon a continuing monitoring of the environment is ascertained and utilized, if policies are enforced, and if they are enforced by the most effective means, if support is high and resistance low in the environment to be changed, and if policy is based upon a comprehensive systems approach to change, rather than a piecemeal attack, then policies will be effective (i.e., attain their goals).

These variables, however, are too general to be useful in producing social change. What are needed are *specific* variables related to these general variables that, if manipulated in a program of social engineering, could increase the effectiveness of public policies directed against racial discrimination and racial inequality. It is the purpose of this chapter to identify a number of relatively more specific variables (although, not specific enough) and to illustrate these with data from the operation of public policy and from empirical research. In addition, specific questions and problems that need empirical study will be raised.

Organizational Efficiency

Policies must be implemented and administered by an organization or organizations especially created or by existing organizations given new functions. In the United States governmental system, these organizations have been agencies and commissions within federal departments and within state and local

57

governments, along with the independent U.S. Commission on Civil Rights. What is at issue here is the degree of internal efficiency of these organizations that have been directed to administer and implement antidiscrimination policies and policies designed to reduce racial inequality.

The first subvariable that can be identified is the degree of *cognitive clarity* of policy among administrators. Cognitive clarity can be defined as the extent to which administrators are clear in their understanding of a policy's goals and of the methods of implementing this policy. This variable can best be illustrated by an example from the Nixon Administration. When George Romney, Secretary of Housing and Urban Development (HUD), was told that he was acting in opposition to the administration's policy in the housing area, Romney was reported to have said, "What the hell is the administration policy? It changes from day to day and hour to hour."[2] As a general proposition, the greater the cognitive clarity of a policy within policy organizations, the greater the effectiveness of policy.

The most obvious example of policy confusion has been in the area of public school desegregation. When the Civil Rights Act of 1964 became law, the enforcement of Title VI in the area of schools was left to the Office of Education in the Department of Health, Education and Welfare. The Office of Education had to decide what were to be the guidelines for integration and when should federal money be withheld from a school district for failure to integrate. The courts had not provided any answers nor did help come from people high in the Johnson Administration. A disgusted superintendent of schools in North Carolina wrote to Commissioner Keppel: "We believe that we are entitled to official written guidelines and criteria for structuring and evaluating compliance documents before proceeding further. We do not want to be unreasonable, but it is our honest conviction that your office is obligated to provide official guidelines to school districts desperately seeking official answers."[3]

The manner in which the first guidelines were finally formulated is a lesson for any student of bureaucracy. Disagreement and inactivity among the official hierarchy of the Department of Education led to an act of initiative on the part of a recently hired consultant—Professor G.W. Foster, Jr., of the University of Wisconsin Law School. Professor Foster wrote a letter on his own to an Arkansas school superintendent stressing what he believed to be legitimate guidelines for integration and then, without official sanction, had the same guidelines published in the *Saturday Review of Literature* on March 20, 1965. Once this article had received wide circulation and had "broken the ice," the Office of Education acted and made Foster's guidelines official policy in April 1965.[4] These guidelines would accept "freedom-of-choice" plans submitted by Southern school districts as long as the school districts made public such choice of schools and did not require complicated forms and embarrassing personal interviews of blacks to discourage transfer. Specific details were given as to how "freedom-of-choice" desegregation plans could be done that would be acceptable to the government. The guidelines were still vague on the issue of faculty integration and on the question of how many grades would have to be opened to possible integration to remain eligible for federal aid.[5]

These were not the only areas of policy confusion. Administrators within HEW disagreed about the application of Title VI to northern schools based upon *de facto* segregation. Some believed that Title VI could be applied whether discrimination was obvious or subtle, *de jure* or *de facto*, while others believed that Title VI could only be utilized if intentional segregation through gerrymandering existed or if proof existed that racial considerations were involved in the provision of demonstrably inferior education for blacks.[6] In October 1965, the Office of Education, without the knowledge of President Johnson, attempted to withhold funds from Mayor Daley's Chicago. The reaction of Mayor Daley, Senator Everett Dirksen, and President Johnson was immediate and intense. A quick settlement was reached in which HEW released funds to Chicago, and the school board merely agreed to reaffirm two earlier ineffective resolutions and to investigate school boundaries.[7]

In a democracy, the degree of cognitive clarity of public policies generally leaves much to be desired due to changing party control of Congress and the Presidency and to changing personalities appointed within the Executive Branch. However, some policies are more confused than others, and little research exists regarding this variable as it relates to the effectiveness of public policy in the area of race relations. Regarding this variable, several interesting problems present themselves: (1) What are the channels of communication and how effective are they between the formulators of policy and the administrators of policy? (2) To what extent do *ad hoc* decisions by administrators and consultants contribute to policy clarity or policy confusion? (3) How is policy clarity affected by changes in party control of the administration or by changes in the leadership of governmental agencies? (4) What are the areas of disagreement and uncertainty among administrators of particular policies within a given agency and between agencies? (5) What subprocesses are involved within government in clarifying a policy? Answers to these questions and to others that could be raised will contribute to our understanding of the relative importance of the degree of cognitive clarity to organizational efficiency and to policy effectiveness, not only in the area of race relations but in other areas as well.

A second variable affecting organizational efficiency is *resources*. Resources include personnel, financial support, and the efficient utilization of these two elements. Government agencies, to be internally efficient, need to have (1) a budget large enough to ensure the employment of competent personnel and to have the financial capabilities of accomplishing assigned tasks; (2) an administrative staff large enough to provide sufficient man-hours commensurate with agency functions; (3) trained and competent personnel with administrative heads of sufficient status and authority to be influential within the larger bureaucratic system; (4) a specialized division of labor with a systematic process of coordination between the divisions to avoid duplication and incompetency; and (5) a system for handling routine administrative matters so that personnel are not burdened by trivia. As a general proposition: The greater the resources available along with their rational[a] utilization, the more efficient the organization and the more effective the policy.

Much of the criticism of federal antidiscrimination policy has been directed toward this question of resources and their utilization. Howard A. Glickstein, of the U.S. Commission on Civil Rights, criticized the Office of Federal Contract Compliance (OFCC) before a Senate subcommittee:

> ... it is clear that Federal contract compliance is not the effective force it should be in assuring equal employment opportunity. Some of the reasons for its failure are readily apparent. One obvious reason is the gross inadequacy of staff. The OFCC, for example, with responsibility for establishing overall policy for all phases of the contract compliance operation, with responsibility for participating in the more significant contract compliance negotiations conducted with individual contractors, and—since May of this year (1969)—with responsibility for conducting five debarment proceedings, has a staff of 12 professionals to carry out these responsibilities.[8]

The largest of the contracting agencies under OFCC is the Department of Defense. The 28,583 establishments that have contracts with the federal government are expected to be reviewed by a staff consisting of 3 supervisors, 13 compliance specialists, and 6 clericals in the central office of DOD, with 140 more members scattered in 11 regional agencies (11 supervisors, 89 compliance officers, and 40 clerical assistants). The U.S. Commission on Civil Rights states that even with an increase in this staff, DOD will not be able to conduct compliance reviews of 50% of its assigned contractors as required in Order 1 of the OFCC, and "judging from past performance, it will be difficult to meet half that goal. . . ."[9] For example, only 8% of the listed defense contract facilities in the southeast region were visited between January 1966 and May 1968, and only about 10% of the listed defense contractors in the entire nation were visited in the one and one-half years before May 1968.[10]

Organizational inefficiency is particularly acute in the Equal Employment Opportunity Commission (EEOC) that was established to administer Title VII of the Civil Rights Act of 1964. "Structural deficiencies have been compounded by acute staffing problems, most notably long vacancies in key positions, and high

[a]As used in the Weberian sense of maximal bureaucratic efficiency and operation.

rates of turnover at all levels, including major policy-making and supervisory positions, and, as a result of meager appropriations, an insufficient number of personnel. Consequently, the Commission has suffered from a critical lack of continuity and direction; its ability to operate efficiently and to fulfill its mandate under Title VII has been seriously impaired."[11] The Office of Compliance (a division in EEOC) has had seven directors in five years; during 1970 it has had no permanent director.[12] EEOC has no uniform or systematic training program for its employees, incompetence is frequent, and its backlog of cases is continually increasing. As of 1970, EEOC has 4,000 investigated cases awaiting some sort of decision, and the number requiring investigation is approaching 2,600.[13] This backlog occurs because it takes approximately two years to process a single case of discrimination; the greatest time lag is in the Decisions and Interpretation Division where a completed investigation often waits 16 to 18 months for a draft decision to be prepared.[14]

With regard to education, the U.S. Commission on Civil Rights in 1967 found that HEW's efforts to desegregate Southern schools was inadequate and that insufficient manpower was a major cause of this inadequacy; yet, on March 1, 1969, the number of HEW professional employees was reduced from 48 to 34.[15]

The most important agency concerned with antidiscrimination policy is the Department of Justice, yet, between 1967 and 1969, there were only 27 attorneys working on exclusively Southern problems covering all areas such as voting, public accommodations, school segregation, and employment discrimination (however, since 1969, twenty more attorneys have been added).[16]

A major factor in the inefficiency of the various governmental agencies involved in antidiscrimination is insufficient funding. "For example, in connection with the 1971 budget request, the HEW Office for Civil Rights asked for an additional 118 contract compliance positions. The Department reduced this request to 95 in its full agency transmittal to the Bureau of the Budget. The Bureau of the Budget cut the new positions to 59, one-half the original Office for Civil Rights request. This was the number included in the budget submitted to Congress."[17] Congress, in the fiscal year 1968, reduced EEOC's request from $7.17 million to $6.65 million. In 1969, a $13.1 million request was pared to $8.75 million, and the 1970 request for $15.9 million was cut back to $12.3 million.[18]

In a general summary of civil rights enforcement made by the United States Commission on Civil Rights relevant to this variable of organizational efficiency, the Commission criticized federal policy on the following grounds: federal policy lacks the leadership of the President of the U.S.; officials responsible for enforcement of the Civil Rights Act often do not have the status and seniority to be influential; only the Justice Department and the Department of Housing and

Urban Development have civil rights officials at the assistant secretary level; agencies have failed to collect or to use data; civil rights goals are ignored, downgraded, entangled in red tape, not coordinated, and even actively opposed within the individual bureaucracies; and the failure to use strong sanctions by the agencies is less a reflection of inadequate enforcement than it is a "triumph of program bureaucrats" where programs have priority over civil rights.[19]

An excellent example to summarize this variable is given by Gary Orfield in his description of the first few months of the administration of Title VI in the Office of Education (1965). Walter Mylecraine, was sent to investigate and improve the Office by the Commissioner of Education, Francis Keppel, and the Deputy Commissioner, Henry Loomis:

Mylecraine . . . was appalled by what he saw. 'Complete pandemonium' prevailed, with everything being done on an ad hoc basis. There was no specialization among the staff, and important southern attorneys and even congressmen were waiting in the halls to try to find someone in authority. No system had been devised to handle the numberless telephone calls and the constant arrival of unscheduled delegations wishing to negotiate with somebody.

The lack of managerial control was particularly evident in the handling of letters from local school officials. Since there was no internal specialization, mail was simply forwarded to whoever had been handling that particular district in the past. With no effective control of the flow of documents through the Office, plans were getting lost in the tide of paper that engulfed the staff and important letters were not being answered. A situation in which one official dealt with one school district while another man of different experience handled its neighbor, and anyone free in the Office might negotiate the problems of either district should a delegation arrive in Washington, magnified the difficulties inherent in the program. No tools were available either to the program's leadership or the Commissioner of Education to find out just what was going on and to effectively direct the operation.

After a day's observation Mylecraine submitted a series of recommendations to Keppel. He called for an immediate doubling of the 30-man staff. He proposed specialization and divided the staff and the files on a regional basis with state subdivisions. Correspondence and incoming phone calls, he suggested, should be centrally controlled. Finally, he sketched a central review operation to supervise the regional negotiating teams and coordinate the work of the program. Keppel gave immediate approval to the revisions. The next day, the Commissioner ordered every operating agency within the Office to supply a quota of personnel until the enforcement of crisis was past. A group of 30 cautious civil servants supplemented the original staff.[20]

A third, and controversial variable, affecting organizational efficiency, is *autonomy*. Price has stated, "Organizations which have a high degree of autonomy are more likely to have a high degree of effectiveness than organizations which have a low degree of autonomy."[21] "Autonomy may be defined as the degree to which a social system has freedom to make decisions with respect to its environment. For example, the typical government agency is subject to external decision making with respect to determination of its budget, personnel policies, and purchasing procedures; in a business firm, none of these issues is decided by groups outside the firm."[22] Besides Price's emphasis on freedom of decision, another element of autonomy is the degree of shared responsibility that a government agency has in effecting particular social changes. Is the government organization the sole agency involved in attempting particular social changes, or do several organizations share in the same responsibility? An autonomous organization will generally be more effective than the more common situation whereby a number of agencies have jurisdictional disputes and often countervailing methods of operation. The Tennessee Valley Authority is an example of a government agency that was relatively autonomous from other agencies in both decision-making power and in responsibility for a set of given policies, and this agency, on the whole, effectively achieved most of its major goals.[23]

Antiracial discrimination policy is now being administered by numerous agencies and departments within local, state, and federal government. Given the nature of the American federal system of government, this is to be expected; however, some degree of consolidation of administration, at least at the federal level, would help to increase the effectiveness of public policy in this area. Within some departments, there are agencies that devote all of their time to racial discrimination, while other agencies in the same department are only part-time administrators (e.g., The Office of Federal Contract Compliance and the National Labor Relations Board, both in the Department of Labor). In addition to the different agencies within various federal departments, there is the United States Commission on Civil Rights, a commission responsible to the President which functions as an investigatory and recommending agency. What is suggested here is that race relations in America are of such a serious magnitude that delegating various aspects of various policies to numerous agencies who may or may not give priority to antidiscrimination is no longer an organizationally feasible approach. What is needed is a semiautonomous federal government organization concerned with racial discrimination and racial inequality (a fully autonomous organization would be politically impossible and democratically undesirable). This organization could have Cabinet status—The Department of Race Relations—and would be concerned with all areas of racial discrimination and racial inequality, consolidating all of the agencies now scattered throughout the departments, and involving all races.

Another possibility, other than Cabinet status, would be the consolidation of all present civil rights agencies into the Commission on Civil Rights. This Commission would be expanded in terms of size, budget, and powers and be akin to another semiautonomous organization, The Tennessee Valley Authority.

Consolidation of either type would be politically difficult, if not impossible, under present circumstances. Not only would the current agencies jealously guard their present bureaucratic kingdoms, but opposition would come from many segments of the American community. Racists of different hues would attack such proposals as fascist or communist inspired. Color-blind liberals would see no purpose in such a large-scale organization that blatantly advertises that the United States is, in fact, a multiethnic and racial society. Others, believing that no racial discrimination exists in America's open society, would see no purpose for one more government bureaucracy. But if America is serious about resolving problems of racial discrimination and racial inequality, which, without doubt do exist, then some form of governmental reorganization and consolidation must take place if public policies directed against such problems are to be more than laws on the books and rhetoric. Stated as a proposition, the greater the autonomy of an organization, the more efficient it will be and the greater the probability of goal achievement.

The Extent of Verified Knowledge Based
upon Continuous Research Programs

The greater the extent to which policy formulators have verified knowledge about the nature of the social conditions and social processes involved in those systems they intend to change, the greater the probability that the policy will have a realistic possibility of success. In addition, those organizations that implement a policy that *continually* monitors and evaluates the social environment that is to be changed, utilizing advanced research methods, will increase their probabilities of goal attainment.

In the area of race relations, we have little highly verified knowledge regarding the causes of racial discrimination, the specific effects of racial discrimination, and what methods are the most effective in reducing or eliminating racial discrimination. Thus, social science can offer little help at this stage to policy formulators. Daniel Moynihan's criticism of social science is probably valid: ". . . social science is at its weakest, at its worst, when it offers theories of individual or collective behavior which raise the possibility, by controlling certain inputs, of bringing about mass behavioral change. No such knowledge now exists. Evidence is fragmented, contradictory, incomplete."[24]

Regarding the second proposition above, few governmental agencies have carried on extensive monitoring and feedback research in their areas of antiracial discrimination programs. Examples of lack of research or inadequate research by governmental agencies are numerous. The President's Committee on Equal Employment Opportunity has been criticized for failure to take regular surveys of minorities in federal employment, for failure to collect data necessary to determine the extent of federal contract compliance, and for its reliance upon reports from contractors themselves.[25] Little data on minorities exists in state and local government employment, hence discrimination in government employment cannot be ascertained in the absence of specific complaints. The U.S. Civil Rights Commission has recommended that all state and local governments keep such data as the numbers and percentages of minority referrals and applications, the numbers and percentages related to the distribution of minorities in the government agencies, and data on promotions, lay-offs, and terminations of minority individuals.[26] In the Department of Agriculture, where Title VI of the Civil Rights Act of 1964 is also implemented, there is little effort to conduct evaluations of the effectiveness of their programs on minority group opportunity or on the extent of equal opportunity compliance with Title VI.[27]

The few instances whereby governmental organizations utilized even a partial research program had favorable implications for policy effectiveness. In the summer of 1966, the Office of Education sent law students to visit school districts in the South, and they compiled a data bank on local conditions so that individual school systems which were once only names could be described in detail. "It became far easier to suggest the particular changes needed in a given division and to effectively plan future enforcement activities."[28] Norgren and Hill's study of state and local Fair Employment Practices Commissions found all but two were largely ineffective in guaranteeing and producing equal opportunity in employment. These two were New York State and Philadelphia. What made these two commissions different from the others was an emphasis on affirmative compliance, greater sanctioning effectiveness (to be taken up under the next variable), and an extensive follow-up research procedure to ascertain the extent to which employers were complying with the law.[29]

The use of research by an organization is particularly important to avoid or to correct unfavorable latent consequences of their programs. A simple example of a latent consequence that was corrected was the fact that federal officials sent to Southern polling booths did not have any observable identification; hence, black voters felt intimidated by these officials. Of a more complicated nature, and one that needs extensive research, is the question of what could be unfavorable consequences of a "discrimination-in-reverse" policy? Gilbert and Eaton have suggested four possible latent consequences of such a policy, if implemented: (1) performance breakdown—minorities that are employed because of their status and not on merit might ultimately fail in their task performance which could lead to validating inferior minority stereotypes; (2) occupational stigmatization—discrimination-in-reverse can be practiced with less risk in occupations that do not require highly technical skills and, hence, the admission of technologically unqualified people into these occupations would eventually lower the status of the occupation; a treadmill effect would be produced in which minorities step up to a higher occupation only to find that this position has depreciated; (3) backlash—from majority group members or "forgotten Americans" disadvantaged by this policy; and (4) erosion of credentialism—if minority individuals can attain a position without the necessary credentials, others will question the value of such credentials.[30] Possibilities of unfavorable latent consequences are always present when changes in human behavior are attempted by organizational action, consequences that could negate the very goals of the policy. A continuing research program conducted by the policy-implementing organizations could forestall or correct such developments and thereby increase the effectiveness of the policy.

One last point needs to be made about the relationship of research and verified knowledge to policy effectiveness. Much research that is currently being done in social science is often superficial and unrealistic (e.g., giving prejudice tests to sociology students). Governmental organizations involved in antidiscrimination policies or in policies directed to reduce racial inequality are in a position to ascertain verified knowledge in a more realistic and intensive manner. They can propose certain social changes, implement these proposals, ascertain the extent of the change, if any, and make further efforts to produce change. Knowledge results from social action. As John Dewey has stated, "The building up of social science, that is, of a body of knowledge in which facts are ascertained in their significant relations, is dependent upon putting social planning into effect."[31] Even in the physical sciences, "Men obtained knowledge of natural energies by trying deliberately to control the conditions of their operation. The result was knowledge, and then control on a larger scale by the application of what was learned."[32] Increases in economic knowledge occurred when government attempted to eliminate a depression. Errors were made and many methods were of little consequence, but even these increased our knowledge. A similar result could be a consequence of governmental efforts to eliminate racial discrimination and inequality.

Enforcement

Public policies directed against racial discrimination obviously must be enforced with sufficient sanctioning power if policy is to be effective. Discriminatory behavior which has been institutionalized, in many cases for several hundred years, cannot be changed merely by passing laws against these practices and norms. Just as discriminatory norms have been enforced by a variety of sanctions applied against both white and black "deviants" in American history, therefore, sanctions must be utilized to enforce *anti*discriminatory norms.

Policies directed against racial discrimination since World War II have included several major sanctioning methods, among these being public hearings, withholding of federal funds, fines after civil or criminal court action, forced acceptance of a minority individual in employment, discipline action taken against employees, cancellation of federal contracts, and in a few cases, the use of troops to secure compliance. Two questions arise—have governmental policies been enforced and to what degree, and, what enforcement methods have been the most effective to date?

The Degree of Enforcement

In the area of housing, with the possible exception of Justice Department action regarding Title VIII of the 1968 Civil Rights Act, little enforcement has taken place. HUD has the power to disbar city governments and private contractors from participating in federal programs if evidence of discrimination has occurred. As of February 1970, *no* debarment proceedings had taken place with respect to discriminatory practices in violation of Title VI (of the 1964 Act).[33] Although HUD is virtually powerless to enforce Title VIII of the 1968 Act (it is enpowered only to use conciliation and persuasion), the agency received 979 complaints in 1969, of which about 100 were successfully conciliated.[34] As of April 1970, HUD had only referred 33 cases to the Attorney-General for prosecution.[35] The Veterans Administration and the Federal Housing Administration have almost entirely relied upon complaint processing. "They have received relatively few complaints and have been of assistance to minority group members in only the comparatively small number of cases brought to their attention. In the few cases in which builders have been debarred for discrimination, neither VA nor FHA impose requirements for reinstatement other than the builder's renewed agreement that he will not discriminate—an agreement he already has violated."[36] Only the Department of Justice has attempted to carry out its fair housing responsibilities. Although the Department has only limited resources, it has initiated suits which can be maximally effective—housing discrimination in large metropolitan areas, cases which may establish precedents, and cases supporting the enforcement programs of other federal agencies.[37] In summary of housing enforcement, a statement by Eley and Casstevens is probably not an overstatement: The function of fair-housing laws has "come to be mainly symbolic and ritualistic. Its existence holds aloft the explicit standard of equal opportunity in housing, confirming the American creed for all of us; but tacitly those who pass the law know that its provisions will not be enforced in a way which basically threatens white neighborhoods. Proponents of fair housing have the public policy they desire, and opponents have the practice they want to preserve."[38]

Federal and state enforcement of policies directed against racial discrimination in employment has been only minimal. In many cases, effective enforcement is limited due to minimal sanctioning power; however, even these minimal powers have not been utilized. The EEOC "is a poor, enfeebled thing . . . (with) the power to conciliate but not to compel,"[39] yet, Section 706 (a) of Title VII of the 1964 Act states that a charge may be filed by a member of the Commission where he has reasonable cause to believe a violation has occurred. To date "no uniform procedures for initiating a Commissioner charge have been adopted, nor has a policy been developed to utilize the Commissioner charge to attack pattern or industry-wide discrimination."[40] The U.S. Civil Rights Commission has stated that the EEOC "is not much closer to the goal of the elimination of employment discrimination than it was at its inception."[41] The Office of Federal Contract Compliance (OFCC) has much greater power to administer sanctions than does EEOC (power of disbarment), yet its enforcement record is not much better. Between 1965 when the OFCC was organized and May 1968, *no* contractor had been disbarred (ineligible for future contracts with the government). Finally, in May 1968, some action was taken. Five proposed debarment notices were sent to five companies (Bethlehem Steel, Timken Roller Bearing Co., Allen-Bradley, B&P Motor Express, and Pullman, Inc.). Two of the companies (B&P Motor Express and Pullman, Inc.) reached an agreement before a hearing was called; Timken reached an agreement after a hearing; Allen-Bradley is being considered for court action; and no decision has been reached as of April 1970 regarding Bethlehem Steel.[42] The Treasury Department, as one of the contracting agencies under OFCC, has avoided the use of sanctions in any form (such as withholding federal deposits from noncomplying banks).[43] Another contracting agency, the Department of Defense, reviewed only 10% of its more than 100,000 contractor facilities in 1969.[44] A major reason for lack of enforcement in this area of federal contracts has been stated by Howard Glickstein, of the U.S. Civil Rights Commission: "Federal agencies are loathe to upset their relations with contractors. Effective enforcement might result in the disqualification of low bidders or other preferred contractors, or cause delays in the letting or performance of contracts."[45]

Antidiscrimination enforcement in education has only been slightly better. In the 1950s and early 1960s, enforcement was primarily left to the lower federal courts acting on NAACP sponsored cases. The U.S. Commission on Civil Rights issued a complete list of desegregation complaints made to their office. These 101 complaints were referred to HEW or to the Department of Justice for action. Of the total of 101 complaints, in only 7 cases was any form of action taken. In many of these cases, HEW or the Department of Justice did not even acknowledge that the complaint had been received.[46] In October 1970, the NAACP filed a suit against HEW on behalf of 25 students in 5 Southern states, charging this department with "general calculated default" of its obligation to enforce laws against federal aid to schools that discriminate. The suit demanded that HEW act against any of the 426 court-ordered districts that have demoted black principals, created segregated classrooms, and have refused to hire black teachers on the grounds of race. In this same suit, the NAACP accused HEW of complete inaction against racial discrimination in Southern colleges and universities, of abrogation of enforcement responsibilities in districts under court orders, of failure to terminate aid to most of the 99 Southern districts that have been accused of failing to carry out HEW-approved desegregation plans, of allowing aid to flow to noncomplying districts for as long as two years after administrative enforcement proceedings were begun, and ignoring accelerated timetables decreed by the Supreme Court.[47]

Failure to enforce antidiscrimination policy in the Armed Forces has been the major factor in racial unrest in the military, particularly in Army bases in Germany. A civil rights committee from the Pentagon, after a tour of Air Force and Navy facilities in England, Spain, and Italy, and Army facilities in Germany, issued a 17-page report in December 1970. The report stated that the most single overriding factor in the current unrest was the failure of commanders to exercise their responsibility and authority in preventing discrimination. Acting on these recommendations, the Secretary of Defense authorized the removal or transfer of officers who fail to produce satisfactory results in dealing with racial discrimination.[48]

Only in the area of voting has there been effective enforcement of antidiscrimination laws. Federal examiners have been sent to selected districts in Southern states to ensure that the Voting Rights Act of 1965 is complied with. Their presence, and the potential threat of criminal action against violators, has been to a great extent responsible for the doubling of black registration since 1965. When coupled with private voter registration drives, the number of blacks registered has been even greater. The following table illustrates the significance of federal examiners in three Southern states.[49]

Enforcement of antidiscrimination laws generally has been absent or only minor. This fact provides a partial answer to an issue previously raised by Tilden LeMelle—whether a racist society can legislate and enforce effective public policy to combat racial discrimination. It has been possible to legislate antidiscrimination policy, but enforcement has been another matter. However, when some degree of effort at enforcement has taken place, what methods have been effective or ineffective? Three enforcement methods will be examined as to effectiveness—individual-initiated court action, government-initiated court action, and governmental organization enforcement.

Table 4-1

Percentage of Blacks Registered to Vote in Particular Counties of the South

	Alabama	Mississippi	South Carolina
Federal examiners present along with voter education project	69.5	51.7	67.0
Federal examiners only	63.7	41.2	71.4
Voter registration project only	57.6	35.9	51.6
Neither (no federal examiners present nor voting registration drive)	45.4	24.2	48.8

Source: United States Commission on Civil Rights, *Political Participation* (Washington, D.C.: U.S. Government Printing Office, 1968), p. 155.

Methods of Enforcement

Individual-Initiated Criminal and Civil Court Action. The least effective enforcement method against racial discrimination is the initiation of *criminal* court action by an aggrieved individual. Only slightly more effective is individual-initiated *civil* court action. Jack Greenberg in *Race Relations and American Law* analyses the inadequacies of these methods:

Experience has shown the inherent shortcomings of criminal laws in the matter of civil rights. Trial has to be by jury, which may very likely be as prejudiced as the defendant; proof must be beyond a reasonable doubt; the statutes must be specific enough to meet the constitutional requirement that a defendant have notice of the alleged defense, leaving room for flexible evasive conduct outside the letter of the law; the burden is on the minority group member to persuade the prosecutor or grand jury to act, and they, at the same time, are preoccupied with the more traditional crimes against person or property. Prosecutions have been few, convictions even fewer.

In civil suits for damages proof need be only by a preponderance of the evidence. But these cases involve jury trials too, as well as the expense of engaging counsel, whose fee is unlikely to be recompensed by the amount of damages awarded, even if they are won. Private suit for injunction avoids the jury aspect of a damage action but is otherwise the same as civil suits for damages. In both of these cases, as in criminal prosecutions, however, the burden of going forward is on the minority group.[50]

Elaborating on the inadequacies of court action, criminal or civil, Denton has cited the facts that expensive and discouraging delays in courts are common, only limited recoveries are permitted, district attorneys are reluctant to prosecute, proof of discrimination is virtually impossible where the discriminator hides his intentions, and each case that has been won does not ensure success in other similar cases by always establishing precedents.[51] This method of enforcement puts the burden of eliminating discrimination on the victims of this discrimination. Even when this burden is alleviated somewhat by legal funds from civil rights organizations (particularly the NAACP), private lawsuits are an inefficient method of reducing racial discrimination in society because enforcement is governed by random suits of individuals seeking redress of some particular grievance. In ten years of suits against Southern school districts from 1954 to 1964, the NAACP with limited resources could only focus on the major cities and the Middle South, and most Southern school districts were never confronted with a challenge to their unconstitutional school systems.[52]

Government-Initiated Court Action. This method of enforcement of antidiscrimination policy is different from the private suits previously mentioned in that an individual complains about discrimination to a government agency and court action is taken against the alleged discriminator in the name of the government. The cost of the court action is borne by the government rather than by the individual or by a private organization, and the action can be brought in the name of the United States or a state, without identifying the person who complained (thus avoiding recriminations).

Because of these factors, this method is more effective than either private criminal actions or private civil actions, but it still generally suffers from a piecemeal attack concerned with rectifying individual grievances (although some cases may result in precedents) and upon the initiative of the victims of discrimination. In addition, such a method means a reliance upon already overworked courts and an enormous expenditure of judicial resources. "For example, Judge Allgood of the Federal District Court for the Northern District of Alabama, wrote an opinion of 157 pages in length in *U.S.* v. *H.K. Porter*, a Title VII suit alleging employment discrimination in a single steel plant."[53]

Enforcement by a Government Organization. The effectiveness of enforcement by a government organization depends, for the most part, upon the type of sanctioning powers available to the organization. If the agency has only the power to use informal methods of conciliation and persuasion (such as the EEOC), then government enforcement will be largely ineffective. Each additional power that an agency has (and, of course, if they are utilized), the greater will be its enforcement effectiveness (such as power to hold public hearings, investigate without individual complaints, issue cease and desist orders, etc.).

The most effective method of enforcement of antidiscrimination policy yet devised to date has been the system utilized by the New York State and the city of Philadelphia's Fair-Employment Practices Commissions. Studies conducted by these agencies involving case-by-case comparisons of postsettlement with presettlement employment patterns revealed that considerable improvement occurred in both the occupational status of blacks and in numerical representation in stores, companies and industries.[54]

The methods utilized by these agencies could be used by state and federal organizations in every field of discrimination, not just employment. And, if ever a consolidated federal race relations department or organization were formed, such an approach to enforcement would significantly increase the effectiveness of public policy directed against racial discrimination. The following are structural and process characteristics of such an envisioned organization, modeled particularly after the Philadelphia FEPC, and upon the evaluations of FEPC's by Michael Sovern:[55]

(1) The organization would have the power to receive and act upon complaints.

(2) The organization would conduct investigations into private and public social organizations where evidence warranted such an investigation (investigation not to be limited by the necessity of individual complaints, however).

(3) If discrimination was uncovered, the organization could issue complaints to the alleged offenders and arrange a conciliation settlement meeting held in private.

(4) The antidiscrimination organization would emphasize affirmative action programs along with the elimination of discriminatory barriers, if the defendant admitted discriminatory practices in this private hearing. A settlement agreement based upon affirmative action and elimination of discrimination would be entered into by both parties. A time limit for this private negotiation would exist (e.g., 30 days).

(5) If the alleged discriminator refused to attend the private meeting or in the private meeting denied the allegations, then a public hearing would be held. This public hearing would require the alleged discriminator to appear by the use of a court order.

(6) In the public hearing, proof would be satisfied by a preponderance of evidence, rather than beyond a reasonable doubt. The evidence would be evaluated by a panel of full-time commissioners whose only function would be the conducting of public hearings (other specialized commissioners would exist for investigation, and for private settlement negotiations in addition to these judicial commissioners). The rights of the defendant would be guaranteed in the hearing, and the right of appeal to the court system would exist. If the commissioners agree that discrimination has occurred, then cease and desist orders would be issued. Cease and desist orders are enforceable in the courts under penalty of contempt of court for failure to desist.

(7) Follow-up interviews and investigations would be conducted by the organization to determine the extent of compliance and to provide educational activities and advisory services for those seeking to comply and those forced to comply.

(8) A judicial review provision would enable private civil rights organizations to take to court cases the antidiscrimination organization has failed to act upon.

If in every case this process reached the public hearing stage, then this method would be cumbersome, expensive, and generally ineffective as an enforcement procedure. However, evidence exists that in the operation of FEPC's with a similar structure, the overwhelming majority of cases were successfully adjusted *before* the public hearing.

In summary of this variable, an obvious, but all important, proposition is: the greater the enforcement of antidiscrimination policy, the greater the effectiveness of public policy. In addition, the greater the reliance upon administrative enforcement utilizing sanctioning powers, the greater the effectiveness of public policy.

Support or Resistance to Policy

The two most obvious *general* factors that relate to policy effectiveness are whether the policy is enforced and how well, and, the extent of support or resistance to the policy. Support and resistance comes from specific targets of policy, from organized groups who see benefits and advantages or threats and disadvantages from the policy, and from elements of the unorganized citizenry. The targets of antidiscrimination policy are generally anybody who discriminates; however, specific targets receive (or are supposed to receive) the major focus of policy. In the United States since World War II, the major targets have been Southern school boards, labor unions, large businesses, companies with federal contracts, real estate agencies, housing development contractors, Southern universities and colleges, and city and state governments (and specific units within the governments) who have enforced discriminatory norms in the past. Specific white organizations have developed or have been reactivated in opposition to such policies, such as the White Citizens' Councils, the Ku Klux Klan, and the John Birch Society. Other predominately white organizations have arisen or increased their activities in support of antidiscrimination—organizations such as the American Civil Liberties Union, B'nai Brith, the National Alliance of Businessmen, and numerous church groups and human relations committees. Of extreme importance has been the support, resistance, and apathy of black people generally, and black organizations, specifically. The most important black groups that have supported or resisted public antidiscrimination policy have been: The National Association for the Advancement of Colored People (NAACP), The Southern Christian Leadership Conference (SCLC), The Committee on Racial Equality (CORE), The Student Non-Violent Coordinating Committee (SNCC), The Urban League, The National Committee of Negro Churchman, The Black Muslims, The Black Panthers, and various Baptist Church committees and organizations. The interaction of all of these forces of resistance and support is a major factor in whatever effectiveness American policy in race relations has had.

Several specific and interrelated variables can be identified that affect the degree of support of or resistance to policies directed against racial discrimination: white self-interest, the activities of black organizations, white prejudice, legitimacy, and enforcement effectiveness.

White self-interest. Norval D. Glenn has written: "Our view is that self-interest is the most basic and important force underlying white policy and action vis-a-vis blacks. Such action more often than not serves the interests of the actors or is accounted for by incorrect perception of objective interest. Values and morals (i.e., the American creed) do under certain conditions prompt and guide the action, but they appear to be powerless to motivate any large segment of whites to action in unison against their perceived interests."[56] In a study utilizing 1960 census data, Glenn concluded that, "the evidence is convincing though not conclusive that many whites in Southern urbanized areas benefit occupationally and economically from the presence and subordination of a large disadvantaged black population. The primary beneficiaries apparently are middle-class Southern housewives and white workers in proprietary, managerial, sales, and upper-level manual occupations. A majority of these beneficiaries apparently have intermediate rather than high income."[57] In a similar vein, Becker and Horowitz have argued that "many whites in civil service positions, in the skilled trades and in similar protected occupational positions have lost or are in danger of losing competitive job advantages as governments act to do something about the injustice that afflicts black communities. Without a general expansion of the economy, which is *not* what blacks demand, injustice inflicted on blacks can be remedied only by taking something away from more favorably situated whites."[58] And in areas such as the South where black deference patterns have been institutionalized, status and self-esteem needs are met, in addition to the economic benefits of subordination.

But self-interest on the part of whites can be a factor in supporting antidiscrimination policies as well as resisting them. For some segments of the white community, antidiscrimination may be advantageous. Before the Populist movement collapsed in the nineteenth century, impoverished whites and blacks cooperated together to improve their economic status. Northern industrialists and blacks benefited alike by the end of the Southern slave system. It has been advantageous for our government in competing with communist countries for influence in the "Third World" to have a domestic antidiscrimination policy. Today, businessmen find that there are profits to be made with black customers. Simpson and Yinger have emphasized this fact of economic interest among merchants in the South: The merchant "may believe in segregation but he also believes in customers. As a result, even in the Deep South, Negroes are beginning to get a minimum of business-oriented courtesy in the use of titles, more nonsegregated services in stores, the right to try on clothing, and the like. In many cities, businessmen and chambers of commerce have taken the lead in supporting 'consumer rights,' that is, the desegregation of all places catering to the general public."[59] A homogeneous "white power structure" dedicated to keep blacks subordinate no longer exists, and efforts by policy-makers and black people to utilize particular interests in the white community can be a significant factor in reducing overall white resistance.

Activities of black organizations. Black action relates to white interests in an interesting manner. Much of white self-interest that benefits blacks is prompted by the increased sanctioning effectiveness of black people generally, and black organizations, in particular. "In spite of the so-called white backlash to the Negro 'revolt,' Negroes are receiving more effective support by whites than they did a few years ago, largely because they have more resources for rewarding and penalizing and are making better use of the resources they have."[60] In other words, the black revolt since World War II has made it the self-interest of many whites *not* to discriminate.

If black people generally, and black organizations in particular, had not by their activities, protests, conflicts, and propaganda made race relations in America a social problem, it can be argued that public policies to reduce and eliminate racial discrimination would never have been formulated, much less implemented. But besides the role of blacks in the *instigation* of policy, what is of particular concern here is their degree of support or resistance to public policies *once initiated*.

The activities and goals of black organizations can be divided into two phases—civil rights and black power. Pinkney summarizes this change:

The civil rights movement was basically reformist, aimed at changing some aspects of the structure of American society insofar as black people were denied some of the rights guaranteed citizens in the Constitution. It was directed toward establishing the principle of legal equality as public policy and toward the responsibility of the federal government in protecting the constitutional rights of citizens. To a degree these goals have been achieved, or, at least, they have been accepted as a matter of principle. The Black Power movement, on the other hand, goes beyond social reform. If the demands for political, economic, and social control by black people over the institutions which are responsible to them, along with the other changes necessary for the "liberation" of American Negroes, are achieved, American society will have undergone revolutionary changes. The civil rights movement did not address itself to the complex, deeply rooted problems facing black people in the slums of the United States. The Black Power movement does. In this sense, the Black Power movement might be said to be the logical extension of the civil rights movement. Where the civil rights movement ended the Black Power movement begins, and it might be said that the death of the civil rights movement gave birth to the black liberation movement.[61]

Antidiscrimination public policy in America has essentially been *civil rights* and integrationist in orientation, and government has not yet taken into account this new development in the form of a new policy.

Under the civil rights phase of the black movement, much of what was accomplished in the reduction of discrimination and inequality was due to black organizations and *not* due to the vigorous enforcement of policy by government. In the area of employment, a few examples illustrate this support. In a study of an FEPA in St. Paul and Minneapolis, Minnesota, all of the St. Paul employers and all but one of the Minneapolis employers credited Urban League pressure in their decisions to break with precedent.[62] The NAACP filed complaints under the new Equal Employment Law in 1961 and broke the historic pattern of discrimination in the Southern industries of tobacco, pulp, textile, and steel, and after a four-year campaign in the Lockheed plant at Marietta, Georgia, they forced the hiring of 200 blacks in skilled categories.[63] In 1964, after demonstrations organized by the NAACP in forty-one cities, General Motors employed blacks in secretarial, professional, managerial, and supervisory capacities for the first time.[64] In every case where barriers were lowered in the petroleum industry, it was due to the activities of black organizations.[65] Prior to the protest demonstrations of various black groups, even the most advanced and effective of FEPC's, Philadelphia and New York state, had failed to take action against the craft unions.[66] CORE, in the summer of 1964, made an agreement with the Bank of America in California to hire 8,000 blacks in the following twelve months, and in the same year forced the A & P stores in New York City to guarantee that 90% of new employees in the next year to be nonwhite.[67] SCLC and CORE in Philadelphia in a selective buying campaign against certain stores opened up 9,000 jobs for blacks in the consumer-goods industries between 1960 and 1963.[68]

In other areas of discrimination, examples may be cited. It was the NAACP in 1955 that demanded that federal aid be denied to schools that did not comply with the Supreme Court ruling (sponsored by Adam Clayton Powell, who attempted to amend every education bill between 1956 and until 1964 when this became policy under Title IV of the Civil Rights Bill of 1964).[69] In a study of housing in Atlanta and Birmingham, it was found that the presence of the Urban League in Atlanta and not in Birmingham made a significant difference in the degree of housing discrimination and inequality in these two cities.[70] In voting registration in the South, it was the presence of an active voter registration campaign conducted by predominately black organizations (coupled with federal examiners) that produced the doubling of black voting registration.[71]

As can be seen by these examples, black organizations until recently have supported government civil rights policy and have been, to a great extent, responsible for any progress that has been made. With the exception of a few older groups such as the Black Muslims, from about the middle 1960s, new organizations dedicated to Black Power have developed, along with changes in the ideology of older groups. What is meant by "Black Power" varies considerably. Black Power may mean black nationalism, increased black ethnocentrism, community control of institutions, increased emphasis on political and economic nonviolent coercion, revolutionary violence, or even "colored self-help." This diversity is significant because a relatively unified black organizational support of government policy no longer exists. For example, in the Spring of 1966, SNCC changed from support of integration to "integration is irrelevant," and opposed the civil rights bill proposed in this year (not passed).[72] In this same year, CORE in its national convention came out for racial separatism and in 1970 officially forsook integration as an effective technique for attaining equal opportunity. CORE has attacked the NAACP and the Department of Health, Education and Welfare in terms of school integration policy. Roy Innis, national director of CORE has stated that school integration is being used to "preserve white control over blacks" by spreading blacks around which weakens their power.[73]

Because of this increased dissent (and possibly the development of a new consensus) among black organizations, current governmental racial policy based upon civil rights and integration will increasingly be even more ineffective than it has in the past. What is needed are studies, on a continuous basis, of the content of black demands, the degree of black alienation, the effectiveness of black leadership, how black demands are processed by governmental agencies, and the possible consequences of such demands upon American institutions.[74] Without such an extensive feedback system, the gap between black demands and policy goals will continue to grow, and public policy may no longer be directed against the elimination of discrimination but the suppression of revolution.

White prejudice. Although overemphasized as a cause of discrimination and as a factor in resistance to changes in discrimination, white prejudice does to some degree affect the extent of resistance to antidiscrimination policy. As has been previously pointed out, the word "prejudice" has a variety of meanings. As used here, prejudice will be defined as *categorical antipathy*, that is, feelings and attitudes of antipathy directed against an entire category of objects (in this case, blacks). Prejudice or antipathy is a variable in that it can vary from mild dislike to extreme hatred.

There are a variety of reasons why individuals develop antipathy toward races and ethnic groups other than their own, and these reasons, depending upon the individual and the social circumstances, may be more or less rational or irrational. Children can learn negative stereotypes of other races that are in a group's culture through the socialization process.[75] Because of a desire to be accepted in a primary or secondary group, individuals will often accept this group's definitions of other races and ethnic groups.[76] Another race or ethnic group can be defined as the *cause* or one's present frustrations and condition or as a *threat* to one's social status (which may or may not be rational; irrational attribution of cause is called "scapegoating" and the irrational perception of threat is called "paranoia").[77] People tend to dislike out-groups that they believe to be significantly different from their own value system.[78] Conflict between ethnic groups or races over scarce values almost always leads to antipathy among the individual members, and this antipathy is positively sanctioned by one's own group.[79] Authoritarian socialization practices by one's parents seem to be correlated with racial prejudice (along with a number of other personality traits such as intolerance of ambiguity, dogmatism, ego-centrism, anti-intellectualism, and a strong emphasis on force and authority in human relations).[80] In addition, the expression of racial prejudice may be useful for an individual to maintain or to attain some position of power and privilege[81] (as George Wallace once stated after losing an election early in his career—"I'll never be out-niggered again.").

This digression into the causes of racial prejudice is relevant to an understanding of prejudice as a factor in the resistance to policies against racial discrimination. As can be seen by the variety of causes, prejudice is not of a single type, and the existence of different types of prejudice necessitates different approaches to reduce prejudice and hence resistance. Most racial prejudice is *normative*. Even with minimal contact with members of out-groups, prejudice can continue in a society because prejudicial expressions are approved by significant others and transmitted by socialization. This type of prejudice can be reduced by programs of education and increased equal status contact with members of other races. This form of prejudice is not deeply rooted in the emotional needs of individuals and will diminish as negative stereotypes are undermined and the expression of prejudice no longer is fashionable or acceptable.

Advantageous prejudice (i.e., prejudice utilized to maintain and attain positions of power and privilege) can be reduced by making prejudicial expressions no longer advantageous. For example, as black voting power increases in the South (i.e., increased participation and bloc voting) election to public office may be dependent upon black support. Expressions of racial antipathy and racism could be detrimental for candidates. This form of prejudice will be reduced in direct proportion of the power of blacks to impose negative sanctions on such behavior. It will be of increasing importance to white self-interest to avoid this form of racial antipathy.

Value discongruence prejudice (prejudice caused by the perception of value differences between races or ethnic groups) will be diminished as blacks gradually achieve proportional distribution in the class system. Historically, blacks and other ethnic minorities were disproportionately distributed in the lower classes, and ethnic cultural variation has always been greatest in the lower classes. Acculturation and mobility became highly correlated, so that with the exception of a few customs and food preferences, ethnic differences within the middle and upper classes are negligible. Much of white prejudice against blacks is based upon an increasing stereotypic view of blacks as lower class (it was not a stereotype around the turn of the century), hence antipathy and resistance to more intimate association demanded by integrationist public policy. Regarding residence, McEntire stated, "It is one thing to ask people of the white middle class to share their neighborhoods with nonwhites of similar income, educational level, and social outlook. It is quite a different thing to ask them to associate as neighbors with people of lower income, education, and cultural standards."[82] Increased equal status contact between blacks and whites coupled with increased black social mobility should reduce this form of racial prejudice.

A minor variety of racial prejudice may be called *pathological prejudice*. In this form of racial antipathy irrational hatred and blame are directed to racial out-groups by personality types characterized by paranoia, insecurity, projection, authoritarianism and closed minds. This type of personality may occasionally seek out others similarly inclined and form groups such as the Ku Klux Klan; however, most of them remain as isolated individuals dispensing their hatreds to anybody who will listen. An example of such pathological antipathy are statements sent to this author by an anonymous anti-Semite: "Mental health and human relations are bold efforts by Jews to brainwash us into accepting red propaganda." "Communism is Jewish—it started in Russia (by Jews from New York). The Russian people are peasants for JEWS, who control Russia. The American people are next in line to be their peasants!" Another example of such paranoic thinking is given by Vander Zanden when a Ku Klux Klan leader stated that there was a conspiracy afoot carried on by blacks, the press, the FBI, Russia, the Nashville school board, the Red Cross, the United Fund, and advocates of polio vaccine and fluoridated water.[83] Similarly, a right wing minister once explained to this author that the blacks, Jews, Communists, Catholics and psychiatrists were engaged in a conspiracy to suppress true Americans; when asked if he had any evidence for such a view, he replied, "No, and that's what's so frightening." There is little social scientists or psychiatrists know that can change this type, but they are not a significant factor in resisting policies against racial discrimination since their power and influence are negligible. Defining this type as "deviant" or as "mentally ill" helps to reduce the effectiveness of their resistance.

Of more importance in this transitional period of race relations in creating resistance to change is a form of antipathy that may be termed *conflict prejudice*. As stated earlier in the section on white self-interest, there are groups and aggregates of white individuals who feel threatened in their newly-won status by the demands of blacks and by governmental efforts to aid blacks. Killian, in his book, *White Southerners* summarizes this source of resistance:

> ... in all regions of the United States the potential for racial polarization and conflict is growing. The socially and psychically mobile white middle class in the South may be especially vulnerable to the status insecurity engendered by the threat of Black Power and the inadequate but much-heralded efforts of the federal government to provide compensatory treatment for black Americans. In this sense a large bloc of white southerners are similar to members of white ethnic groups in the North who, having just climbed from the bottom rungs of the social ladder, feel their new status threatened by the aggressive demands of blacks and the sympathetic response such demands receive from a secure white elite. Together these threatened people may become the source of a new wave of political reaction in a nation that required radical solutions for the problems of its minority of poor people, yet cannot persuade the affluent majority to accept such solutions. These people, who can hardly be called "new rich" but rather "recently poor," constitute a special kind of minority group, insecure, defensive, and potentially aggressive.[84]

In a stable or a declining economy, these "recently poor" groups are threatened by actions and programs designed to raise the status of blacks; this is *not* an irrational perception on the part of these whites. This form of racial antipathy can, however, be reduced in an expanding economy where both whites and blacks make gains.

These distinctions between types of racial prejudice and their relationship to policy resistance have not been empirically examined either in community studies or on the national level, and this should be another area of research to be included in a more comprehensive UNITAR study of American race relations. What we do have are a number of national surveys or community studies that summarize, by percentage, agreement or disagreement to a number of statements that *may* indicate prejudice or lack of it. For example, in the *Newsweek* surveys by Harris, it was found that in 1963, 51% of the respondents objected to having a black neighbor, with this percentage declining to 37% in 1965. In 1963, 17% of the white respondents objected to working next to blacks, and this declined in 1965 to 10%.[85] Another example that gives a little indication of white prejudice and changes over a five-year period are the items asked in the Harris surveys of 1963 and 1968 (see Table 4-2).[86]

It will be argued later that vigorous and consistent enforcement of antidiscrimination policy directed toward behavior should take priority over efforts at attitudinal change; however, prejudice does relate to discrimination and to resistance to antidiscrimination policy. If longlasting changes in racial behavior are to be expected, efforts to diminish prejudice should *accompany* programs of social control.

The legitimacy of public policies. Although the issue of "illegitimacy" is often a cover for self-interest and/or racial prejudice, in many cases it is not. In any event, the definition of a policy as legitimate or illegitimate is an important factor in the degree of resistance and support to a policy. Groups and segments of the population vary as to consensus on the "rightness" of particular public policies. What is legitimate to one group or segment may be illegitimate to others. Disagreement may occur over general policy *goals*, over policy *methods* of implementation, or over the legitimacy of *organizations* empowered to utilize particular methods. As a general proposition—the greater the consensus on all three of these elements of a policy in a society, the less the resistance, and the greater the effectiveness of the policy.

Table 4-2

Percentage of Whites Agreeing to Statements about "Negroes" in 1963 and 1968

	1963	1968
Negroes have less ambition than whites	71%	67%
Negroes want to live off handouts	41	49
Negroes have less native intelligence than whites	39	44
Negroes breed crime	35	33
Negroes are inferior to whites	31	24
Negroes are asking for more than they are ready for	71	67
Negroes are more violent than whites	x*	42

*Not asked in 1963.

Source: Adapted with permission of the publisher from William Brink and Louis Harris, "What Whites Think of Negroes," ed. Raymond J. Murphy and Howard Elinson, in *Problems and Prospects of the Negro Movement* (Belmont, California: Wadsworth Publishing Co., 1968), p. 26.

Since World War II, most whites accept the legitimacy of equal opportunity, equal rights, and equal protection for blacks as *general* principles. For example, the Brink and Harris survey in 1963 found that 93% of whites nationwide and 88% of Southern whites approved of the right of blacks to vote; 88% of whites in the country and 75% of Southern whites approved of the unrestricted use of buses and trains; 82% of white nationally and 75% of whites in the South believed that blacks should have decent housing; and on the principle of equal opportunity in employment, the figures were 88% and 80%, respectively.[87]

But there are two major problems in accepting such findings at face value (besides wondering about the nature of the minority that does not approve of these rights). The first problem relates to one of generality. Does acceptance of general and abstract goals of racial equality translate into specific equalitarian behavior and belief? The evidence from one study indicates that it does not. Frank Westie, in a study done in Indianapolis, found that the percentage agreeing with general value statements declined when general values were translated into specific racial situations (see Table 4-3).[88]

A second problem with accepting this relatively high consensus on general equalitarian principles is the fact that a large number of Americans do not believe that racial discrimination exists. For whites to accept equalitarian principles does not necessarily mean that they believe that blacks are denied these rights, or that these are goals to be *pursued*. For many whites, these principles are accomplished facts; the fact that blacks are unequal in many areas is the fault of blacks, themselves, not an undemocratic system. Campbell and Schuman's study of fifteen cities in 1968 found that when whites were asked why blacks have worse jobs, education and housing than whites, 56% believed that this inequality was mainly due to blacks themselves, 19% said that it was mainly due to discrimination, and 19% believed inequality was due to a mixture of both factors.[89]

Possibly due to the fact that many whites do not believe that racial discrimination exists and to the belief that legal methods cannot or should not be utilized to change racial behavior, the percentage of whites accepting the legitimacy of governmental *legal efforts* to eliminate racial discrimination declines significantly from the high consensus on *general principles*. In the same Brink and Harris survey of 1963, 57% of whites nationwide and 31% of Southern whites approved of a federal vote-enforcement law (compared with 93% and 88%, respectively, who approved of this right); 66% of nationwide whites and 29% of Southern whites approved of a public accommodation antidiscrimination bill (88% and 75% for the right); 62% of whites nationally and 40% of whites in the South approved of the federal fair employment practices law (88% and 80% for right of equal opportunity).[90]

All of the previously cited legal efforts of the federal government to reduce racial discrimination were of the first type of public policy previously mentioned (i.e., civil rights protection). When two other types of public policies are

Table 4-3

Percentage Agreeing with General and Specific Valuation Statements

General Valuation Statement	Percentage Agreeing	Specific Valuation Statement	Percentage Agreeing
Everyone in American should have an equal opportunity to get ahead	98	I would be willing to have a Negro as my supervisor in my place of work	60
All people should be treated as equals in the eyes of the law	98	If I went on trial I would not mind having Negroes on the jury	76
Children should have equal educational opportunities	98	I would not mind having Negro children attend the same school my children go to	79
People should help each other in time of need	99	If a Negro's home burned down, I would be willing to take his family into my home for the night	64
Everyone should have equal right to hold public office	91	I believe that I would be willing to have a Negro representative in the Congress of the United States	71
Each person should be judged according to his own individual worth	97	I would not mind if my children were taught by a Negro school teacher	67
I believe in the principle of brotherhood among men	94	I would be willing to invite Negroes to a dinner party in my home	29
Public facilities should be equally available to everyone	83	I would be willing to stay in a hotel that accommodates Negroes as well as whites	61
Under our democratic system people should be allowed to live where they please if they can afford it	60	I would be willing to have a Negro family live next door to me	35
I believe that all public recreational facilities should be available at all times	63	I don't think I would mind if Negro children were to swim in the same pool as my children	38

Source: Adapted with permission of the publisher from Frank R. Westie, "The American Dilemma: An Empirical Test," *American Sociological Review* 30 (August 1965), 527-538.

involved—using "affirmative action" methods or "discrimination-in-reverse" methods—the percentages of whites who accept the legitimacy of these methods again significantly declines. In a study of 6000 people in six major cities in 1967 by the Lemberg Center for the Study of Violence at Brandeis University, 66.2% of whites approved of blacks and whites having equal job opportunities; 38.1% of whites approved of on-the-job training by industry so blacks not fully qualified could be hired; 27.2% of whites approved of special governmental training programs for blacks; 7.2% of whites approved of giving blacks a chance ahead of whites in promotions if they have the necessary ability; and only 3.5% of whites approved of giving blacks a chance ahead of whites in hiring for jobs that blacks have not had in the past.[91]

Although the evidence is scarce, a decreasing *scale of legitimacy* seems to exist for whites. The great majority accept the legitimacy of equal rights and equal opportunity; a sizeable majority (about two-thirds) approve of government efforts to guarantee equal rights and equal opportunity; approximately one-third of whites accept the legitimacy of affirmative action; and only a small minority approve of "reverse discrimination."

This is one type of decreasing scale of legitimacy. Another would be based upon social distance in which the more intimate and extended the interrelation between black and whites envisioned by a public policy, the less the legitimation of such a policy. Such a social distance factor is probably the major reason for white hostility to busing as a method of integrating schools and to open-housing laws, although other values such as "neighborhood schools" and "private property rights" are invoked in opposition. In 1967, a nationwide Harris poll found that whites were opposed 3 to 2 to fair-housing laws,[92] and, in addition, every popular referendum on fair-housing up to 1968 has produced defeat for such policies.[93] Busing to achieve integrated schools has met with severe resistance in almost every community where it has been tried and to the defeat of many political candidates advocating such a method.

It should be understood that legitimation or normative consensus regarding public policy is not fixed and can change significantly by social events. The House of Representatives in April 1963, summarily defeated antidiscrimination amendments on two education bills after five minutes of debate on one and ten on the other.[94] But in May, in Birmingham, Alabama, the confrontation between Martin Luther King, Jr. and Sheriff Bull Conner occurred. The television coverage of the moral atrocities that ensued "sent surging energy through the civil rights movement across the country and generated the national anger that made basic change possible."[95] "Suddenly the President (Kennedy) sensed that the country was ready to accept a wide expansion of Federal power into such vital areas as protection of equal access to public accommodations and examination of employment discrimination"[96] as well as in education. It was this event along with the assassination of President Kennedy that made possible the passing of the Civil Rights Act of 1964. However, the riots that occurred in the summers of 1965 and 1966, again produced a change among whites regarding public policy. A Gallup Poll in 1966 indicated that 58% of white Americans felt that the Administration was moving too fast on civil rights issues.[97] A white backlash had begun. In terms of school integration, Orfield states the implications of white backlash: "By summer's end (1966) there was no political mileage left in the integration issue. The civil rights movement was in confused retreat, and the public consciousness was filled with vivid images of rioting Negroes chanting 'black power.' The great wave of energy and commitment to racial justice had crested. . . ."[98]

Blacks generally have higher approval rates than whites for limited civil rights policies, affirmative-action policies and discrimination-in-reverse policies, but there is a similar decline in legitimacy among blacks. In the same study by the Lemberg Center for the Study of Violence, 70.8% of nonwhites (predominately blacks) approved of equal job opportunities for blacks and whites; 61.1% approved of on-the-job training by industry so blacks not fully qualified could be hired; 42.5% approved of special government training programs for blacks; 19.3% were in favor of giving blacks a chance ahead of whites in promotions if they have the necessary ability; and 13.2% approved of giving blacks a chance ahead of whites in hiring for jobs they have not had in the past.[99]

The majority of blacks in the United States still accept the legitimacy of government policies based upon the attainment of civil rights and an integrated society and reject the more extreme Black Power programs of some organizations. In the 1965 Harris Survey, blacks 47 to 1 believed that the Civil Rights Act of 1964 would bring further progress in all areas, and integrated schools were desired by a 6 to 1 majority. In this same year, 64% of the respondents preferred racially mixed neighborhoods while 18% did not.[100] In the Campbell-Schuman study of fifteen cities in 1968, 48% of blacks preferred mixed neighborhoods and another 37% stated that racial character of neighborhoods makes no difference; only 13% preferred an all or mostly all black neighborhood. These respondents rejected black nationalism 19 to 1 (however, 6% or an estimated 200,000 blacks in 15 cities were in favor). They were asked whether they approved or not of various black leaders. Black leaders that have supported public policy were generally approved of, while militant Black Power advocates were not (91% approved or partly approved of Martin Luther King, 62% approved or partly approved of Roy Wilkins—35% did not know enough about him to say one way or the other; 35% approved or partly approved of Stokely Carmichael—30% did not know enough about him; and 27% approved or partly approved of H. Rap Brown—28% did not know enough about him). A major conclusion emerging from the Campbell-Schuman study is that most blacks are in favor of maintaining a group identity, but they are not in favor of rigid social separation of the races (psychological and cultural pluralism but not structural or social pluralism). Even the majority accepted the "American Dream"—78% agreed that a young black who works hard enough can usually get ahead in this country in spite of prejudice and discrimination (93% of the college-educated agreed with this).[101]

As has been mentioned, time and events can change views about the legitimacy of policy, and this holds true, of course, for blacks as well as for whites. Lack of significant progress along with rising expectations triggered by some future act of white violence could drastically change this present support of policy by the majority of blacks. Already considerable disenchantment with the effectiveness of the federal government has set in. Polls in 1963, 1966 and 1969 show a drastic drop in the percentages of blacks that believe the federal government has been helpful to black rights—from 88% in 1963, 74% in 1966, to only 25% in 1969.[102] Not only does legitimacy affect policy effectiveness, but policy effectiveness affects legitimacy.

As is apparent, considerable research is necessary in the area of legitimacy, an area that is relatively easy to ascertain by present survey methods, and yet is still quite fragmentary. What is needed is a more comprehensive and continuing survey program (ideally carried on by our proposed semiautonomous governmental organization). The following are some of the major problems that need to be ascertained from both white and black respondents:

1. beliefs about general American values (without racial reference);
2. beliefs about equal rights for blacks—generally;
3. beliefs about equal rights in specific areas—housing, employment, etc.;
4. beliefs about the extent of discrimination generally and in specific areas;
5. attitudes of whites about blacks in specific situations (e.g., would you sell your house to a black?) and vice-versa (would you sell your house to a white?);
6. attitude toward use of federal government to pass laws against discrimination and to enforce these laws—generally;
7. attitude toward state and local government involvement in antidiscrimination policies, generally;
8. attitude toward general methods of attaining equality in America—civil rights, affirmative action, and reverse discrimination;
9. attitudes regarding federal and state governmental policies in specific areas such as housing, voting, schools, etc.;
10. attitudes about *particular* governmental policies (including goals, methods, and implementing organizations)—for example, FEPA and FEPC;
11. attitudes regarding poverty elimination programs; and
12. attitudes about Black Power programs.

Although some data exist on many of these problems, what is necessary is that *all* of these questions be asked of *each* respondent. If this is done, then some interesting relationships between the items may emerge—for example, a person may believe in equality, not believe that discrimination exists, and be opposed to governmental antidiscrimination programs for this reason; or, an individual may accept the fact that racial discrimination exists, approves of governmental intervention, but varies according to what methods are appropriate in particular areas.

In addition to ascertaining attitudes and beliefs regarding these problems among *individuals* of both races, the degree of consensus within a particular *group* is an important problem (e.g., CORE, the American Legion, The National Association of Manufacturers, NAACP, the United Auto Workers, etc.). Groups vary as to their power and influence over public policy, and ascertaining legitimation consensus within and between groups may be more useful than general public opinion surveys. Finally, we need to know what is the degree of normative consensus about particular policies within governmental agencies that implement the policies.

Knowledge about such problems related to legitimation, on a continuing or periodical basis, will significantly improve the effectiveness of public policy directed against racial discrimination.

Enforcement effectiveness. Two major ideas are to be presented here. One is the idea that consistent, vigorous, and legitimate social control methods significantly affect human behavior; and the other is the fact that the American system of government is peculiarly incapable of such consistent, vigorous and legitimate social control procedures (or, in other words, effective social control can drastically reduce resistance, and the American governmental system enhances resistance).

Several social psychological studies exist that have stressed the significance of legitimated social control in affecting behavior. In one study (Pepitone and Wallace, 1955)[103] the experimenters asked their subjects to sort out the contents of a wastebasket containing assorted and often disgusting debris. The subjects did so without strong protestations. In another experiment, Martin Orne and his associates[104] gave subjects 2,000 sheets of simple additions to be computed with the instruction—"Continue to work; I will return eventually." This was sufficient to make them work for several hours. They were even told to tear up each sheet of additions into 32 pieces and throw them away after completion, which they did, also without significant resistance. This author has had introductory students in a sociology class stand on their heads, make faces, and do exercises simply because the students were told to do so. But the classic, and most immoral, of such experiments was done by Stanley Milgram.[105] Subjects who believed they were involved in an experiment on learning, administered electric shocks (the electric machine did not actually shock confederates of the experimenter) to people because they were told to do so. If the subject asked about injury to the victim, the experimenter replied, "Although the shocks can be extremely painful, they cause no permanent tissue damage." Twenty-six of the forty subjects pulled the "generator" switch up to the maximum 450 "volts." One mature and poised businessman became a nervous wreck, twisting his hands, and on one occasion stating, "Oh, God, let's stop it." Yet he continued to obey the commands of the experimenter to the very end.

Most people are law-abiding (or more specifically, rule-abiding) and will conform to constituted authority, regardless of personal predilictions. When German officers and officials expressed during the Nuremberg trials that they were following orders, this was not significantly different from American soldiers following orders at My Lai in Vietnam. However our liberal orientations make us appalled at such behavior, enough evidence does exist that such is the case.

What specifically is involved in this conforming behavior? William Gamson argues that, "Perhaps the most powerful and common means of social control is simply the conveying of expectations with clarity and explicitness coupled with clear and direct accountability for the performance of such expectations. As long as legitimacy is accorded in such situations, individuals will regard their noncompliance as a failure and any interaction which makes such a personal failure salient is embarrassing, unpleasant and something to be avoided."[106] ". . . the desire to avoid the embarrassment of being derelict under surveillance is a powerful persuader."[107]

These factors of clarity, explicitness, accountability, and legitimation which produce conforming behavior can be illustrated in race relations. If clearly defined policies against racial discrimination are enforced with vigor and with consistency by legitimate authority, individuals responsible to this authority will not discriminate. Vander Zanden elaborates on this principle in regard to school desegregation:

Desegregation that proceeds by unequivocal, resolute steps backed by responsible authorities tends to be more readily accepted and taken for granted than a halting desegregation that appears unsure of itself. Where desegregation is firmly administered, people tend to concede the legitimacy of the policy, although they may not abandon anti-Negro sentiments. A general expectation of resolute authoritative intervention, for example, of the invocation of laws against violence, incitement to violence, and truancy, decreases the probability of open conflict. This generalization has been consistently supported by evidence gathered in race relations studies and in desegregation experience.[108]

When the national management of Southern companies imposed a policy of desegregation and nondiscrimination (imposed on the national management by governmental and black organization pressure), "in virtually all instances the transition from discrimination and segregation to equal opportunity and integrated employment took place smoothly and without any manifest resistance on the part of white workers."[109] Of interest is the example of two plants in the same Southern company that utilized different methods.

One Southern plant was headed by an authoritarian Southern gentleman who received his orders and carried them out. He called his plant superintendents together and said, "Gentlemen, we have these instructions to integrate and we are going to do it. There will be no difficulty, it will just be done." A superintendent spoke up and remarked that he was a Southerner and just did not think he could work in such a situation. "That's fine," said the plant manager, "we will give you two weeks' pay." The superintendent changed his mind. Another superintendent said, "What will happen if some of the men get in a fight with these new colored recruits?" "I'll fire the people who are fighting, I'll fire their foreman, and I'll fire the superintendent of the group."

Integration took place speedily and without incident. "We don't like it, but we are living with it," one superintendent told the writer.

In another plant of the same company, the man in charge was a well-trained graduate of a human relations-oriented business school. He saw the integration task as a fine case study for his alma mater and invited a team of professors to observe and to advise him. He began a long education process, hired local sociologists, consulted with the branches of the Urban League and the NAACP, and carefully indoctrinated all his people. The result was a walkout, much difficulty, problems of supervision, and general turmoil. The job of integration still remained to be accomplished six months later, but the manager had by then been replaced.[110]

Some business concerns have polled their employees regarding their opinions about hiring black workers in higher status positions. Dean and Rosen,[111] and others argue that this is the worst possible method. Instead of introducing changes in a matter-of-fact way defined as legitimate by the management, polling the employees means that these workers are being asked to define the situation themselves. In such a situation, the employees fall back upon their prejudices, and resistance is created.[112]

In the examples given, and one could add the military services where integration and nondiscrimination have been accomplished by fiat, there are direct lines of responsibility from the highest authority level to the lowest member of the hierarchy. The less this *direct* responsibility occurs, the less the effectiveness of social control in creating social change, and direct control is not a characteristic of the American governmental system.

Although the central government of the United States has increased its power, authority, and area of concern since the turn of the century, the federal system of government is still permeated by localism which enhances resistance. State and local governments possess extensive powers, and "states' rights" still is a factor questioning the legitimacy of extended centralized controls. For example, in the area of school desegregation and discrimination, the 1954 Supreme Court Decision was resisted on the grounds that it was unconstitutional, in arguments similar to the doctrine of nullification utilized before the Civil War (laws passed by the central government which oppose the rights of a state can be declared "null and void"). In this same area of schools, the power of the states made resistance possible through the passing of laws to delay or to prevent integration. By 1957, at least 136 new state laws and new state constitutional amendments had been passed in the South for just such a purpose. "The most common device was the pupil assignment law, giving local school boards power to establish criteria for assigning students. By manipulating the various requirements, local officials could generally preserve segregation. State laws made the process more expensive and lengthy for black applicants by creating elaborate administrative procedures. Thus each Negro student had to clear a set of high hurdles before he could appeal the predictable ultimate rejection (of the laws) to the Federal courts."[113]

There are numerous other factors which enhance resistance to any policy of the central government. Congress controls the funds and the legislative apparatus for any national programs, and Congressmen are highly influenced by local concerns and interests. The seniority system in Congress has enabled extensive Southern control over the various congressional committees due to the lack of a viable two-party system in the South. Departments of the Executive Branch must depend upon these committees for the funds to carry out their programs. Changing administrations and changing members of the various departments of government at the federal level make difficult a consistent and clear policy over an extended period of time. The multiplicity of governmental units in the United States are admirably suited to prevent vigorous and consistent enforcement of a national policy. If, for example, a city or an enclave within a city, passes a fair-employment law or a fair-housing law, one can simply move to a nearby area that has no such laws. Fair-housing laws in a central city can have the latent consequence of *increasing* segregation through the movement of whites to suburbs where no such law exists.

Obviously, if the preceding proposition is correct, a centralized authoritarian governmental system can control behavior and produce changes far more effectively than can the American system. This is not to argue for such a totalitarian approach to race relations, but if one is concerned only with the *effectiveness* of policy, direct and consistently enforced policy will produce changes.

American government, through its systems of checks and balances, is suited for resisting change rather than promoting it. Orfield illustrates this structural characteristic of American government at the level of the national Congress:

Only twice in American history has Congress been able to forcefully protect the rights of Negro citizens: in the decade following the Civil War and, for a moment, in the mid-1960s. The first was made possible by the subjugation of the South and the creation of an extraordinary political situation. The second rose from the irresistible force of a great tide of public anger (following the Birmingham incident). The first ended when the public grew weary of contention and turned against the black man and when the political power of southern whites became crucial once again in national politics. The great reforms disappeared, leaving few traces for generations (around 1900). In late 1966 it became obvious that the strength was gone, at least for a time, from the second wave of reform.[114]

This second effort was made possible only by a temporary coalition of unified northern and western states along with divided border states. This coalition made possible the passing of the Civil Rights laws of 1964 and 1965, but "by the end of 1966 this coalition was only a memory, and southern power began to assert itself."[115]

Given these structural characteristics of American government, it is difficult to see any consistent and vigorously enforced social control apparatus at the federal level. Perhaps, as Tilden LeMelle has stated, all that can be hoped from the federal government is a framework of legitimation through which blacks themselves will put pressure upon the leadership of the numerous private and public organizations and institutions in American society. When a change to antidiscrimination is perceived to be in the interests of these various elites, they can change the behavior of their directly responsible employees, bureaucrats and underlings in the manner outlined above. In a pluralistic democratic society, such an approach (as opposed to national social control) may not only be the feasible pragmatic approach, but the only approach normatively desirable.

The Comprehensiveness of Policy

The final general variable to be examined which relates to the effectiveness of policies directed against racial discrimination and/or racial inequality is the degree of comprehensiveness of the policy—that is, the degree to which a policy envisions and utilizes a "systems" approach to social change rather than a "piecemeal" attack.

Human behavior does not consist of a number of isolated and disconnected acts, but it exists within a web of social interaction or social systems. The "parts" of any given social system are, in turn, social systems—a number of social units within the larger whole. A society is a large social system which itself is part of such larger units as civilizations and total human society. Within a society, such as the United States, numerous subsystems exist such as institutions, organizations, communities, social classes, social movements, culture complexes, and social situations. At another level of analysis, one can conceptualize such subsystems as the political, the economic, the religious, the educational, etc. Each of these parts or subsystems are more or less interconnected with all of the other parts in the sense that behavior in one area has consequences for behavior in other areas. In addition, changes in one part produces, in some degree, changes in all other parts, even if human social systems are not as finely interconnected and interdependent as are mechanical, biological, ecological, and cybernetic systems.

In terms of such a concept as "system," racial discrimination does not exist in isolation from other aspects of society, nor does one area of discrimination (e.g., housing) exist separate from other areas of discrimination (employment, education, etc.). And, with the exception of an *analytical* division, racial *discrimination* cannot be separated from racial *inequality*, since the two are interdependent. To break into such a network, one can postulate that *if* racial discrimination took place only in education, such consequences as the following would exist: educational discrimination creates low levels of education and job skills; low education and employment training means low-status occupational positions; low-status occupational positions create low income and minimal social power within the race; low income means a low level of subsistence and a lower level of health, since health in America is greatly determined by one's ability to pay; poor housing results from low income and poor areas receive only minimal services from municipal governments; any decrease in employment rates affects unskilled and semiskilled workers more drastically; unemployment, low income, and crowded housing is related to family instability and disorganization; powerlessness creates apathy symbolized by low voting rates; in addition, powerlessness, low status, and relative deprivation can produce higher crime rates when crime is perceived as a method of adjustment to stress, etc. One could continue with such an analysis examining other consequences and interconnections produced only by racial discrimination in education, but the point is clear; and racial discrimination is not limited to education in the United States, as we have seen.

Today, America is a highly complex and interdependent network of social behavior. Regionalism is diminishing as the culture of the United States becomes more standardized due to mass communication, mass transportation, and large organizations which transcend regional barriers. One does not have to be a Marxist to appreciate the primary significance of economic factors in producing such an interdependent system. It is for this reason that any policy combating racial discrimination must, simultaneously, attack the consequences of past discrimination which have produced racial inequality, and, this means change in the economy. As Greenberg has stated, "A rule ending Jim Crow higher learning is limited in realization if colleges are overcrowded. . . . Removing bias from hiring signifies little in a depression or a tight job market. . . . Ending exclusion from housing does not count for much if there are few homes or apartments available."[116] Similarly, Marshall has written, ". . . one of the reasons many civil rights leaders are disillusioned with the state FEP laws is because they assumed that the laws would cause significant changes in racial employment patterns. Employment patterns are not, however, determined mainly by the laws, but, rather, by a host of factors, only one of which is discrimination. Changes in racial employment patterns are much more likely to respond to general expansion in employment, improvements in education and training, manpower policies to improve labor mobility, job forecasting, and employment counseling. Indeed, antidiscrimination legislation is likely to be most effective if it is considered as a part of general manpower and employment policies."[117]

If public policy is only concerned with eliminating discrimination (i.e., intended choice restrictions), then a comprehensive program conducted simultaneously against all forms of discrimination with sufficient sanctions will be more effective than a "piecemeal" approach. If, however, a policy is designed to eliminate the unequal effects of *past* racial discrimination (which also limits choice) along with *present* discrimination, then a far more comprehensive program is necessary. A policy conducted against both racial discrimination and racial inequality must consist of a comprehensive three-pronged attack that "advances on all fronts." The first program would be concerned with the elimination of the present barriers through law enforcement. The second aspect would center around "affirmative action." Organizations would be encouraged (and in some cases, forced) to active measures in addition to merely the negative elimination of barriers. Without sacrificing "technological" criteria, colleges would actively recruit members of minority races, businesses would set up employment contacts in black communities, overly restrictive technological criteria (such as a high school diploma) could be waived with the substitution of more extensive on-the-job training, private and government scholarships should be given to potentially capable minority students, etc. The third phase (all three conducted simultaneously) would be essentially concerned with a nonracial elimination or reduction of class inequality and the improvement of American communities. Since blacks are disproportionately distributed within the lower socioeconomic strata and within the more depressed areas of cities, this third phase would, however, benefit them more than whites in terms of proportion, but not, of course, in terms of absolute numbers.

This third program has to be far more comprehensive and massive in scale than any approach utilized today or in the past (such as Model Cities or the War on Poverty). S.M. Miller and Frank Riessman, in their book, *Social Class and*

Social Policy[118] have developed a series of specific policy goals for a comprehensive and systems approach to class inequality. Their goals are summarized below:

1. Increase the income levels of the poor with adjustments for familial and area differences along with maintaining the stability of this income.
2. Increase the pension reserves of the poor.
3. Eliminate the stigma of public assistance by providing adequate income in ways that are not demeaning to the individual.
4. Provide a system of liquid reserves at twice the current income of a family with the ratio of savings going down as income rises; provide a minimum level of a liquid reserve (e.g., $3,000) in the form of cash, bank deposits, liquid stocks.
5. Develop a program of adequate housing for every American.
6. Provide neighborhood amenities in terms of a minimal level of density of housing, open areas per individual, fire and police services, and garbage pick-up.
7. Provide a physician for every 700 persons with underwriting of all health costs along with medical programs for early identification of medical problems.
8. Develop neighborhood service centers (decentralization) such as consumer rights programs, health services, legal rights, educational and tutorial programs, family planning, mental health services, public welfare, job training and placement.
9. Increase the college graduating achievements of children of the poor—with an interim goal of a rate of college graduates among the poor being 50% of the rate of the nonpoor.
10. Development of school programs and procedures to involve "dropouts" for example, a second-chance university with experience being given educational credit.
11. Increase the use of nonprofessional manpower to aid teachers, particularly with some drawn from the ranks of the poor.
12. Integrate the schools with a simultaneous increase in funds for all such target schools.
13. Provide low-cost public transportation.
14. Eliminate the differential treatment of the poor by the police and by the courts.
15. Provide protection from bureaucratic policies and practices with an ombudsman, intervener and expediter—utilize people from the ranks of the poor who have been highly trained for such a role.
16. Increase the participation of the poor in programs that affect them and

provide for self-determination of such policies—not only in poverty programs, but in the conduct of such agencies.

17. Formulate programs to increase the voting rates of low-income groups—decentralization of voting offices, year-round registration, longer voting and registration hours, and voter registration drives.

Some such program with massive public financial aid will be necessary if racial inequality is to be drastically reduced and an increasing "crisis in black and white" is to be diminished. Broom and Glenn have written, "Only a massive program of education, job retraining, and occupational up-grading—on a scale far greater than anything now proposed by Negro leaders, the Federal government, or any agency or organization concerned with Negro welfare and status—can save the majority of Negroes from many more decades of inferior status."[119]

To summarize, five general variables, each with several specific subvariables, affect the degree of effectiveness of public policies. Maximal utilization of each one of these variables will increase the probabilities of effective policy against racial discrimination and racial inequality.

5 Summary and Conclusions

Discrimination may be defined as differential treatment by members of a dominant social category which functions to deny or to restrict the choices of a subordinant social category. Discrimination of some form always takes place when one category of human beings is in a subordinant position to another social category due to a difference in social power. Discrimination is the result of a power differential and cannot be changed without changing this distribution of power.

Differential treatment involves three elements—norms, techniques, and sanctions. Discriminatory norms are proscriptive and prescriptive expectations of behavior which limit the alternatives available to a subordinant group in given spheres of social activity. Techniques are specific methods of implementing the norms which may be overt and direct or covert and indirect. A single norm—such as "Negroes shall not vote,"—can be implemented by a number of techniques such as poll taxes, literacy tests, personal intimidation, etc. Sanctions are the rewards and punishments invoked by members of the dominant social category to secure compliance of subordinant individuals to the norms (and, on occasion, to secure compliance by members of the dominant category to respect these norms).

The most effective system of discrimination would be one in which there were no challenges to the norms and no necessity for negative sanctioning due to the acceptance of the legitimacy of such a relationship.

In stable systems of human relationships, discrimination is institutionalized and is not conceived of as a social problem (i.e., negatively evaluated) but is viewed as part of the moral order. Only when such systems of human interaction are undergoing change, do they come to be defined as problematic.

Racial discrimination involves a relationship between dominant and subordinant social categories called races—human beings set apart by a few perceived physical variations, particularly skin color. Racial discrimination functions to maintain the disproportionate distribution of races within a society's stratification system (classes or estates), creating different life chances and life styles for members of these races.

In the United States, black-white relations have taken the form of two types of racial stratification, with one form succeeding the other. The first system was one primarily based upon a slave-free status relationship which began in the

American colonies in 1619. Between 1619 and approximately 1750, this system gradually became institutionalized into one of the most severe patterns of dominance and subordination ever developed. The discriminatory norms were total, restricting the black slaves in all areas of behavior, the techniques of implementation were direct and overt, and the negative sanctions imposed on violators were severe. The doctrine of biological and moral inferiority (racism) legitimated this system.

The Civil War and Reconstruction terminated this first system of racial stratification, and after the federal troops were withdrawn from the South in 1877, the second system gradually emerged by 1900.

In both the North and the South, this new system was characterized by mixed overt and covert techniques of discrimination, a strong emphasis on racial segregation (apartheid), and a more competitive pattern of race relations. In the South, racial discrimination and racial segregation was more total and comprehensive than in the North, although it was less a total system than was the slave system. The Southern pattern placed more emphasis on formal norms (i.e., laws) and extensive informal norms to maintain the system than did the North. In both regions, *racism* continued to be elaborated on by politicians, theologians, and scholars as the major ideological legitimation of this second system; however, a new ideology also accompanied racism and was gradually developed in this period. This new ideology was based on the belief that America was an open society, and that black inequality was due to low motivation which made them unable to take advantage of this open system of opportunity. This meant that whites increasingly denied the reality of racial discrimination.

Beginning during World War II and up to the present time, this second system is being transformed into a new pattern of race relations, although what this new pattern will be is not yet clear. There have been at least nine major social change factors operating to produce this transformation: (1) employment opportunities created by the war; (2) changes in the economy; (3) increasing urbanization of blacks; (4) decline in the political power of the Southern Democratic Party; (5) the emergence of the United States as a world power; (6) nationalism in Asia and Africa; (7) social science developments which have begun to undermine the doctrine of racism; (8) the increase in black competitive ability and black power; and (9) the development of public policies directed against racial discrimination.

Focusing on this ninth factor, public policy, four general types of public policy designed to reduce and eliminate racial discrimination *and* social inequality can be identified. The first type may be called *"civil rights"* policy and is concerned with the elimination of the discriminatory barriers by guaranteeing equal rights for all citizens. In this type of policy, the assumption is that the elimination of the barriers (i.e., discrimination) will, as a consequence, diminish racial inequality in time. The second type policy may be termed *"affirmative action."* Policies of this nature attempt to influence or to force targets to take positive action by giving preference to qualified individuals of minority races and to seek out such individuals. This "affirmative action" is in addition to the elimination of the barriers to equal opportunity. The third type of policy involves "discrimination-in-reverse." Minority racial status is the sole criteria for membership or employment and members of the dominant or majority race are discriminated against. Both the second and third forms of public policy may or may not use a quota system. The last type of public policy focuses on the reduction of "class inequality" without specific reference to racial factors. Since, by definition, subordinant races are disproportionately distributed in the lower classes, racial inequality will be reduced as a latent function of such a policy. Of course, a "civil rights" policy must accompany such a program to eliminate discrimination.

Public policies since World War II have primarily been of the first type—"civil rights," and in some instances "affirmative action." In addition, under the Johnson Administration and the Nixon Administration, the fourth type of policy has been initiated—particularly the "War on Poverty" and the "Model Cities" program.

There has been some change since World War II in some areas of racial discrimination and racial inequality and little change in other areas. The following are the extent of change in racial discrimination and racial inequality in major areas since World War II:

(1) The ratio of nonwhite to white median family income has changed little since World War II; nonwhite income remaining approximatley one-half that of white income.

(2) Blacks have made significant gains in the intermediate occupations between 1940 and 1960, but there has been only a negligible increase in the higher-level occupations.

(3) Blacks have made substantial progress toward proportional representation by position and by vocation in the Armed Forces, particularly, the Army and the Air Force; however, at the highest levels, the change in proportional representation has been minimal.

(4) Since 1955, segregation in labor unions has declined drastically, and formal and overt racial discrimination has virtually been eliminated; however, informal and covert techniques still exist in many unions, and there has been little change in the building trades unions with only token black representation.

(5) There has been only minimal change of black representation in law enforcement agencies, with only token representation, at best, in the South.

(6) Racial desegregation of public schools in the South between the end of

World War II and 1964 has been negligible (1% of all black students in integrated schools) with a slight increase by 1968 (15% of all black students in integrated schools); in the nation, as a whole, school segregation is increasing.

(7) The number of years of schooling completed by blacks almost doubled since 1940, and the ratio of nonwhite years of schooling to white has been reduced.

(8) School desegregation in the South has meant the loss of status or of employment for many black educators, and segregation of faculties and of students within "integrated" schools has developed.

(9) Residential segregation by race has remained virtually the same since 1940.

(10) Real estate discrimination since World War II has changed from overt and direct techniques to covert and indirect techniques which are equal to or superior to those of prewar discrimination.

(11) Black voting registration has increased significantly since 1940, although it is not yet proportionately equal to white voting registration (from 4% of all eligible black voters in 1940 to 60.8% in 1968).

(12) Although some forms of overt and direct political discrimination exist in the South, new forms of covert and indirect discriminatory techniques have been developed, but these are not as effective in preventing black political participation as earlier methods.

(13) There has been a slight increase in the number of black state and federal legislators with black legislative representation still far from proportional.

Public policies directed against racial discrimination vary as to effectiveness. Effectiveness, the dependent variable, may be defined as the degree to which policy goals are achieved. Five general variables can be identified which relate to policy effectiveness—internal organizational efficiency, research, enforcement, support and resistance, and the comprehensiveness of the policy. Within these generic variables, several relatively specific subvariables can be related to policy effectiveness in the form of propositions:

(1) The greater the cognitive clarity of a policy, the greater the efficiency of organizations implementing the policy and the greater the effectiveness of the policy.

(2) The greater the extent of organizational resources and their rational utilization, the greater the organizational efficiency and the greater the effectiveness of policy.

(3) The greater the autonomy of an organization, the greater the efficiency of the organization and the greater the effectiveness of policy.

(4) The greater the extent to which policy formulators have verified knowledge about the social conditions they intend to change, the more effective the policy.

(5) Organizations that continually monitor and evaluate the environment that they are attempting to change, particularly the manifest and latent consequences, if any, of their programs, will have a greater probability of goal attainment.

(6) The more organizations attempt to introduce changes into an environment, the more social change knowledge is increased, and with the utilization of this knowledge, the more effective the policy.

(7) The greater the sanctioning power (of policy-implementing organizations) that is utilized in enforcement of policy, the greater the effectiveness of the policy.

(8) The greater the reliance upon minority-initiated criminal and civil actions against discriminators, the less the effectiveness of public policy.

(9) The greater the reliance upon government organizations that have the power to investigate, to hold hearings, to issue cease and desist orders if compliance does not occur, and to enforce their decisions (i.e., use force), the greater the effectiveness of policy.

(10) The greater the extent to which policies can serve particular self-interests in the dominant community, the less the resistance to the policy and the more effective the policy.

(11) The greater the power of minority group organizations and their active support and enforcement of a policy, the more effective the policy. The greater the dissensus and factionalism among minority group organizations over a public policy, the less the support of the policy and the less the probability of policy goal attainment.

(12) The greater the racial prejudice within the majority race, the greater the resistance to antidiscrimination policy and the less the effectiveness of the policy (however, there are different types of prejudice which call for different strategies to reduce this form of resistance to policy).

(a) The majority of individuals in a dominant racial group are prejudiced because the prejudice is positively sanctioned, it is normative, and it is transmitted from generation to generation through socialization. Resocialization programs and increased equal status contact between individuals of both races can effectively diminish this form of prejudice and hence reduce resistance to public policy.

(b) Prejudice which is advantageous in attaining or maintaining a position of privilege and power can be reduced by making it no longer advantageous through actions by government and by minority group activity.

(c) Pathological prejudice found in a minority of individuals can be diminished as a factor in resistance to policy by efforts to isolate these individuals through the process of defining them as deviants and by preventing their access to positions of power and influence.

(d) Another form of prejudice, conflict prejudice, will increase as particular marginal groups within the majority race are threatened by minority efforts to raise their status. This form of prejudice, and hence, resistance can be reduced by an expanding economy where members of both races in conflict can gain.

(13) The greater the consensus on the legitimacy of policy goals, policy methods, and policy-implementing organizations, the more effective the policy.

(14) In the United States, at least, legitimacy declines from a high concensus on the elimination of barriers to equal opportunity, to policies based upon affirmative action, and discrimination-in-reverse is perceived as illegitimate by the great majority of Americans. Other things being equal, policies based upon reversed-discrimination will encounter severe resistance and, hence, the less the probabilities of the effectiveness of such a policy.

(15) Because the great majority of human beings are rule-abiding, a policy instigated by legitimate authority and characterized by clarity, explicitness, and direct accountability will be effective.

(16) The greater the emphasis on a combined systems approach involving both the elimination of racial discrimination and the reduction of class inequality, the greater the probabilities of reducing racial inequality. If the goal of a policy is the reduction of racial inequality, then the elimination of racial discrimination is necessary but not sufficient to accomplish this end.

At the present stage of social science, and particularly, the present stage of research into race relations, these propositions are, of course, in the nature of hypotheses to be examined, rather than propositions that have been scientifically verified.

Public policy directed against racial discrimination and racial inequality in the United States is one of several factors that have produced social change in race relations since World War II. If one could weigh the relative effects of all of the factors creating racial change, public policy would be ranked lower than most. Many of the policies have been unclear and have changed with administrations. Agencies established to enforce policy have been scattered throughout various federal departments, lacking leadership of sufficient status to be influential. Budget allocation and personnel resources have been highly inadequate. With the exception of the U.S. Civil Rights Commission, little research and data collection has been done by the various state and federal agencies. There has been too much reliance upon leaving the enforcement of antidiscrimination laws to the victims of discrimination in the form of private legal action in the courts. Although the sanctioning powers of government in this area are far from powerful (withholding funds, fines, criminal action, and public hearings), they could have effect if citizens knew that they would be utilized; however, the major cause of the relative ineffectiveness of public policy to produce change has been lack of enforcement. With very few exceptions, these sanctioning powers have not been utilized. Little effort has been made by governmental leaders to systematically recruit the support of powerful white segments of society whose interests could be served by antidiscrimination and the reduction of racial inequality. There has been no nationwide campaign to reduce racial prejudice; this has been left to understaffed and underfinanced local human relations organizations. Few black leaders have been brought into governmental service to implement policy, and government has failed to maintain a continuous feedback system with the black community. What knowledge of black interests and views of policy that have been ascertained have been done by a few private organizations on an incomplete and sporadic basis.

In addition to further examination of the sixteen propositions related to policy effectiveness, other problems for further research have been raised in this book and are restated below:

1. What is the extent of formal and informal discriminatory norms in particular organizations and in particular communities today?
2. What kinds of discriminatory techniques are being utilized, if any, in particular organizations and in particular communities?
3. How is it possible to measure the degree of effectiveness of racial discrimination? The degree to which a discriminatory norm is adhered to by members of a dominant race and subordinate race? The reasons why members of a subordinate race do not challenge the norms? The degree of success of the intent of the norm (e.g., voting rates)? The number of times a norm is violated and sanctions are imposed?
4. Is it possible to find two similar communities where the difference in discrimination is great and thereby be able to ascertain the effect of discrimination on inequality, as opposed to other factors?
5. Is it possible to ascertain a pattern of sequential effects of racial discrimination in one area upon other areas as suggested by Wilbert E. Moore?
6. Are beliefs such as racism major determinants of racial discrimination or are they post hoc legitimations of racial discrimination? Or is there some particular pattern of interaction between these two variables?
7. How can a social scientist ascertain the existence of and the extent of covert discriminatory techniques and informal discriminatory norms?
8. Is the common practice using data of racial inequality (e.g., occupational distribution, membership rates, unemployment rates, educational attainment, etc.) as proof of the existence of racial discrimination a valid procedure? What other factors could produce this inequality?
9. Does the significance of racial prejudice in affecting racial discrimination vary according to specific social situations or types of social activities? For

example, is prejudice more of a causal factor in affecting discriminatory behavior in relatively unstructured social situations and social activities, as opposed to highly structured social conditions?

10. What is the effect of racial inequality upon racial discrimination (as opposed to the other way around)? For example, does discrimination lessen as a group achieves greater proportional representation in the stratification system?

11. Do discriminatory norms which are covert and informal become overt and formal when a minority race enters areas of social life which they have never previously entered? Do discriminatory norms emerge where there were none previously when this occurs? Do formal overt norms change to informal and covert when a minority race increases its challenges to these norms?

12. How effective are the channels of communication between the formulators of public policy and the administrators of public policy?

13. To what extent do the daily decisions of administrators contribute to policy clarity or policy confusion?

14. How is the degree of policy clarity affected by changes in the party control of the national administration or by leadership changes in the governmental agencies?

15. What is the extent of disagreement, uncertainty and alienation among administrators of public policy?

16. What are the processes involved within government in clarification of a policy?

17. What priority is given antidiscrimination compared with other duties and programs in governmental agencies (agencies established to specialize in antidiscrimination and in agencies not so designed)?

18. To what extent are the activities of different governmental agencies contradictory or countervailing in the area of race relations?

19. What are the sources of resistance to a unified and semiautonomous department of race relations?

20. What is the content of black demands?

21. What is the degree of black alienation?

22. How effective is black leadership?

23. How are black demands processed by governmental agencies?

24. What are the possible consequences of black demands upon American institutions?

As was stated in the introduction, this book has been a preliminary examination of a major project, and the results, proposals, propositions, and concepts presented are at best tentative.

Appendix A

Guidelines for a Study of the Effectiveness of
Policies and Measures against Racial Discrimination

UNITAR has prepared this paper for the Teheran International Conference on Human Rights in the hope that it will encourage and assist further research and studies by individuals and institutions on the effectiveness of measures against racial discrimination. There is an urgent need to undertake more studies in this area. The harmful and tragic effects of apartheid and other forms of racial discrimination have been realized and acknowledged by the international community and measures have been taken in many countries to combat racial discrimination. Declarations and discussions by the United Nations and other international organizations have promoted concern and remedial action. Even though this has resulted in many descriptive and analytic studies of aspects and manifestations of racial oppression and prejudice, in reviewing the whole field of investigation, one is made keenly aware of the need for comparative research concerning the effectiveness of measures against racial discrimination.

UNITAR has, therefore, undertaken a research project whose basic purpose is to ascertain and compare the effectiveness of measures and policies against racial discrimination in a number of countries. By analyzing the racial and ethnic conflicts in typical societies with varying economic and social conditions, and by assessing the effectiveness of different types of measures and policies adopted and implemented by governmental units and private organizations, it will be possible to obtain important insights into the interplay of factors which determine the existence and character of racial problems. It could furthermore provide much needed information about those mechanisms by which antidiscriminatory measures make their impact on society.

This is a cross-national research project, involving a number of country studies. The first country study has just begun in the United Kingdom, in cooperation with the Institute of Race Relations, and arrangements are being made for other country studies. The different country studies will provide the basis for the comparative evaluation.

The research methodology which UNITAR is following and which is now presented to the Conference may be considered a substantive contribution to this field. Its significance is twofold: first, it is a pioneering research project in the area of comparative studies, especially for evaluation of the effectiveness of measures against racial discrimination; second, it will serve as a stimulant and a partial methodological model for other country studies. It should be possible to

This report was prepared by the United Nations Institute for Training and Research and submitted to the International Conference on Human Rights, 29 February, 1968.

approach a variety of similar multinational studies on human rights in much the same way. We feel that the methodology of the UNITAR study is no less important than its results.

UNITAR considers that many other studies with similar objectives are urgently required in order to understand and evaluate measures against racial discrimination and other curtailment of fundamental human rights leading to the adoption of more effective action. It is for this purpose that UNITAR presents in the following pages a description and detailed design of the comparative study of effectiveness of measures and policies against racial discrimination. The International Conference on Human Rights may wish to recommend to scholars in all countries the need for further studies in this area. UNITAR, for its part, would be prepared to provide information and assistance in the formulation of research methodology appropriate to each country and situation.

Description of the project

The study will analyze and compare policies and measures to combat racial discrimination and the results obtained in national societies. It will study the racial situation in national societies in order to evaluate the effectiveness of such policies and measures, and compare them with spontaneous factors in the dynamics of the whole structural situation as sources of change in the patterns of race relations. It will not, however, endeavor to describe the whole area of race relations in the country studied.

The study will cover situations involving various ethnic categories, and will look at the problem in different economic, political and social contexts, degrees of national development and geographical areas. The collection of data and the field work of the teams to be established for the purpose in various countries, may follow common guidelines detailed in the present paper. This will assure basic comparability of various national reports.

It is necessary that each national society to be studied must have: (a) a multiracial population; (b) a significant degree of tension between the ethnic groups, and (c) some accumulated experience in concerted action against discrimination. The societies should be located in different geographical areas, present a diversified set of ethnic constellations, and should be at different stages of social, political and economic development.

In the contemporary world, the problem of racial discrimination has new and extremely complex dimensions. It is no longer restricted to the level of interpersonal relations—the small group, the neighborhood, the local community—but is developing in a broad national and international context, affecting relations between sovereign States. Furthermore, the most important issues today with regard to racial problems, at the national as well as at the international level, are the product of intentional and deliberate actions by organized groups. Thus, the proper study of the problem of racial discrimination nowadays requires a study of the sociology of majorities, and the methodology reflects the fact that today racial discrimination is occurring in some sociological and political contexts without historical precedent.

In other words, what we would like to analyze and to comprehend with regard to each national society under study, are the respective importance and weight of (a) the policies and methods deliberately used; and (b) the dynamics of the structural change itself, in determining the intensity and direction of the trends prevailing in the patterns of racial relations from World War II until today. The present situation will be approached as the historically accumulated result of the effectiveness or lack of effectiveness, of the policies applied and the methods used during the last quarter of a century to build desirable patterns of racial relations in the society under study.

An attempt should be made to extract, from the analysis and comparison, possible guidelines for better performance in the future. To a great extent, it will be a study of the social structure of multiracial societies, of the social values, and of the different types of social action that are causing multidirectional change in prevailing models of interethnic relations.

Objectives of the study

In the structure of any national society, there is a system of roles and functions to be played by individuals and groups of individuals, in different spheres of life. The criteria and the actual distribution of groups in different social positions, and the attribution to them of different social roles, are, at any given moment, the accumulated result of historical processes of social conflict and accommodation. In multiracial societies, ethnic traits frequently become the support and justification for imposing and maintaining criteria of social differentiation. To understand how and why, in the societies under study, social differences are expressed in racial terms, what is the role played by intentionally applied measures in changing these patterns, and what are the other influential factors that arise spontaneously from the dynamics of the situation itself—these are basic goals of the projected study. The research procedures recommended in this paper are designed in the light of these goals.

"Race," "ethnic group," and such terms will, for the purposes of the study, be taken with the meaning they have in the everyday life of the society concerned, independently of qualifications scholars have made regarding the scientific meaning of these terms. In every society, these words express the perceptions of the groups involved concerning their similarities and differences; and the patterns of actions nad reactions we propose to study are based on such perceptions and definitions.

Research at the National Level

National studies

The national study to be prepared will result from extensive fieldwork—six months, at the minimum. The national studies could be used as the basis for a comparative study for a region, continent or the whole world.

Any national study should make:

(i) an objective characterization of the situation existing at the end of World War II;
(ii) an analysis of the factors and trends that, up to the present, have acted to change that situation; and
(iii) the identification and evaluation of the role played by the deliberate application of policies and measures to combat racial discrimination, compared to other influential factors.

Data required

The collection of basic data in each society under study will be along the following lines:

1. *Structural characteristics of the multiracial society*: demographic data; position of the groups in the stratification system.
2. *Main traits and trends*: historical background and analysis of the origins and orientations of the patterns of values, assumptions and goals connected with the prevailing racial policies.
3. *Policies and measures*: analysis of the policies and measures applied to combat racial discrimination.
4. *Successes and failures*: assessment of the effects and evaluation of the results of the policies applied, compared with other factors connected with the dynamics of the racial situation itself.

It should not be inferred from the detail with which the working hypothesis is outlined below that it involves a number of in-depth studies of racial relations. Although it will deal with the background and setting of the problem, the comparison and evaluation will be centered on the effectiveness of measures against racial discrimination.

Structural characteristics of the multiracial society. *Demographic data.* When the racial situation in country A is contrasted with the racial situation in country B, it is important to know that in A the minority group is represented by some thousands of people while in B the minority constitutes 10 million or so. Furthermore, the social role of a "minority" may, in fact, be performed by a majority of a given population. The demographic background of the social structure in which the patterns of interethnic relations are established must therefore be analyzed as the starting point for any further approach to the problem. The basic sources of this information are the national censuses and equivalent demographic registers. The last national census made before World War II and the most recent national census will be compared to characterize the main trends of the structural changes that have occurred.

Statistics on migratory movements will be analyzed to identify the influence of migrations upon the ethnic profile of a national population. Emigration will be also considered as an attempt, forced or spontaneous, to reduce tensions. For these purposes, the points of origin and destination, and the ethnic, social, national and other characteristics of migrants must be taken into account. Internal migrations connected with racial tensions, with changes in the political status of the country, or fostered by changing economic patterns, deserve special consideration with regard to their present implications as well as for the future.

The same applies to vital statistics: birth rate, mortality rate, infant mortality rate. Data on ethnic differentials *in causa mortis* obtained from reliable sources (even if only sample studies and/or covering only some periods of some groups) as well as other equivalent data concerning population structure and dynamics, may when duly analyzed illuminate many aspects of the social organization within which the interplay of racial relations occurs.

Partial populations represent "samples" selected by the very functioning of a given social structure, and their analysis may be extremely pertinent for the study. For instance, the ethnic composition of the penitentiary population, the military, the teaching profession, the highest bureaucratic layers, and so forth, represents a set of relatively accessible information because it is usually collected for other purposes. When subjected to systematic analysis and interpretation, such information may throw light on many aspects of the structure of a multiracial society.

Special consideration must be given to the analysis of data relating to mixed groups: origins, definition, composition, social status. The same applies to data concerning "passing" through the racial line.

Position of the groups in the stratification system. In any multiracial society, ethnic differences are not the only social differences between the groups. From this starting point, many essential clues may be explored, all leading to the very core of the subject of the study. The basic problem here is to discover the nonethnic cleavages among the ethnic groups using different social indicators.

In many instances, the sources of information are the same as for the demographic data, but in other cases, the number and quality of the sources are more diversified. The following points should be mentioned with regard to the indicators to be used in the study:

Income. The goal here is to obtain a breakdown of national levels of income on an ethnic basis, in order to learn the relative location of the groups on the economic side of the social pyramid.

The sources of this information may vary from country to country: internal revenue data, insurance companies' figures, statistics of wages and earnings, labor statistics, etc. The breakdown will be made into five levels of income, so that in a group of 100 individuals at each level, it will be known how many are of ethnic group A, B, C, etc.

Occupation. Here, aside from giving an indication of the types of activity, information easy to find in printed sources, the goal is to obtain specific information concerning the usual way each of the various ethnic groups make their living. Such information, even when existing in official sources, often is released only on request. In some countries, information is collected concerning the position in the occupation (i.e., employer, employee, autonomous, etc.). On the other hand, in some countries, for various reasons, no breakdown is made or available according to ethnic origin. In certain cases, the solution may be to obtain special processing from the original sources. The purpose is to identify in objective terms the trends and the amount of ethnic concentration in various clusters of the occupational structure of each society.

Education. These data are, perhaps, easier to obtain. The tables to be drawn up will present, by ethnic origin, indices of literacy and the termination of study at the primary, secondary and college levels. Whenever possible, a table will be added concerning the ethnic origin of the student population and the holders of diplomas of higher study. Here again the intention is to identify some clusters in the prevailing educational pattern and to learn the reasons for their configuration as well as to try to understand the factors causing change.

Power. Under this heading, we need information concerning the ethnic composition of the bodies performing decision-making functions: (i) Parliament, house of representative or governing collegiate bodies (national and local, when pertinent); (ii) collective governing bodies (council of ministers, cabinet, etc.); (iii) higher civil servants, senior military personnel, governing bodies of political parties; (iv) heads of more important banks, corporations, universities, newspapers, broadcasting stations; (v) the judiciary and the religious hierarchy; (vi) other pertinent information concerning the social differences between the various ethnic groups in relation to power and the sources of power. The patterns of relations of the political parties and groups with the main racial issues in the societies concerned will be analyzed here.

Common sources of this information, aside from official statistical publications and registers, are "Who's Who" books, social registers, chambers of commerce, clubs and associations, etc. In the presentation of information and data concerning this item, it is particularly important to indicate, in each case, the criteria of the selection of people for these functions, and the implications, actual or potential, of these systems of social position over the processes of ethnic relations.

Patterns of mobility and segregation. In the structure of any multiracial society, two aspects deserve special attention: *status*—meaning the position in social space; and *situs*—meaning the position in physical space. In interpreting the data concerning demographic aspects, status scales, etc., particular attention must be given to the prevailing patterns and trends of social mobility with regard to the various ethnic groups as well as to changes during the period under review. As far as the geographical distribution of ethnic groups is concerned, we will define segregation as a pattern of relative isolation within a social structure, in which the spatial distribution of ethnic groups reflects social distances between them.

An index of segregation may be applied, of course, not to the national territory as a whole, but to the smaller areas in which "minority groups" are more concentrated, especially in urban areas. Knowing the percentage representation of each ethnic group in the total population of a scale for each district (or ecological area) can be prepared. At one end of the scale, the proportion of each group in each district would be the same as their proportion in the total population of the area, random distribution; while at the other end of the scale, the pattern would be one in which the total population of each group is concentrated in one and the same district (or ecological area). Variations along the scale will indicate variations in the index of segregation. This is only one method. Other suitable indexes may be adopted.

The final goal of the collection and interpretation of data concerning the multiracial social structure of each society under study is to have a clear idea of the profile and dynamics of the position and role of the various ethnic groups. For this purpose, other information and data may be added to the abovementioned, according to its availability in each society. As a rule, all sources for the figures and tables included in national reports must be fully and explicitly indicated.

Main traits and trends. Any social tension has its "natural history"; and the understanding of this history is an essential prerequisite for the analysis of the tension itself. A part of each national study should be devoted to the historical background of the existing racial tensions in the society under review. To a great extent, the figures collected for the first part will make sense only if and when projected on the screen of the historical background.

We are not, of course, interested in an exhaustive and full account of all the small factual details. On the contrary, we must be selective, concentrating our attention more on an intelligent interpretation of significant relations between facts and trends than on detailed description *per se*. This is the only way to obtain an illuminating background for understanding the objective data and to obtain an insight into the dynamics of the whole situation.

The following set of questions may be taken as a general guideline to the historical survey:

(a) How old are these problems in the society under study?
(b) What have been the main stages of their evolution?
(c) Earlier patterns of racial relations contrasted with prevailing patterns;
(d) Main trends appearing between World War II and the present day.

Special emphasis must be given, in the historical survey, to the analysis of: (i) the changes occurring at different institutional levels of the national society; (ii) the changes of the status of the nation in the structure of international society; (iii) the nation's relation to, or reciprocal influence on, changing patterns of racial tension, discriminatory practices and the application of policies to combat them. It goes without saying that this applies equally to changes for better as well as to changes for worse, the important thing being to learn the how and the why of whatever trends are observed.

A basic and guiding hypothesis here, which would be tested in the historical survey, is that: In any society in which social positions are ethnically marked, prejudice and discrimination are fostered when qualitative changes occurring in the social structure threaten established patterns, and the groups having a dominating position in the prevailing social system react, expressing in racial terms their social resistance to change.

On the other hand, this hypothesis alone could not help us in the study of some contemporary manifestations of racial tensions as for example where and when racism, or racialism, or any form of race consciousness appear, not as a factor of resistance to change but as one of the basic ingredients of an emergent nationalism and as a strong emotional motivation to promote change and to stimulate economic, social, cultural and political achievements.

"Sociological imagination" must be fully exercised here to develop the procedures for this part of the investigation: Content analysis of documents, statements, newspapers, humor; formal and informal interviews with people; participant observation in the daily life of professional, recreational, educational, political and other kinds of associations; "life-cycle" or biographies of representative individuals strategically located in the framework of the racial patterns under study. These will provide the necessary insights.

The aim of this part of the study is not necessarily to discover new facts, but to analyze, for the period under review, the interplay of the racial problems and the racial policies and ideologies at different levels and in different environments, and their patterns of mutual conditioning.

It would be appropriate to attach to the study essential documents such as biographical sketches, photographs, newspaper reports, and statements to illustrate and support the interpretations offered in the text.

The policies and measures adopted to combat racial discrimination in any society are based on certain assumptions, resulting from an implicit or explicit definition of the situation, and they also imply a set of goals to be reached. It is in relation to these values, assumptions and goals that an evaluation of the effectiveness of these policies should be made rather than in relation to any ideal model superimposed by the observer on the situation under study.

What are the targets of the existing "racial policies?" Complete assimilation, aiming at an ethnically homogeneous society in the future? Nonconflicting coexistence in a mosaic pattern? Complete separation and domination by one group over the other? Other models could be offered as examples.

How are these policies and measures perceived by the groups that practice discrimination as well as by the groups discriminated against? How are these perceptions manifested in actions and reactions on the part of the groups involved?

It is a common pattern in these situations of intergroup tension that, aside from the main groups confronting each other, there is almost always a "third party," the "others," whose perception or definition of the situation frequently does not coincide with that of the main conflicting groups. It is important to know who they are and how they function, bearing in mind that in such situations the "third party" position is a social role.

The attitudes and reactions of the groups discriminated against, their opinions concerning the usefulness of the measures, the alternatives they offer, their position as spectators or their active participation in the promotion of the policies, must be observed as counterpoints to the discriminatory ideologies and must be studied in depth.

The patterns of internal solidarity of a group against which discrimination is practiced is another important aspect to be studied. These depend upon many factors such as the numerical strength of the group, the fact of having or not having the same nationality as those practicing discrimination, the location of the group in the stratification system, etc. The internal segmentation or stratification of the group discriminated against according, for instance, to lines of elites and masses, rich and poor, older and younger generations, lighter or darker color, etc., seems to have definite importance in the formation of different value-orientations and perceptions inside the same ethnic group. Special consideration should be given to this problem in order to identify subgroups inside each confronting group—e.g., "black bourgeoisie," "poor whites"—and to analyze how the internal social stratification of each group as the specific role of each segment impinges on the development of the situation as a whole.

In this context, special attention must be given to the *elite sectors* of the groups discriminated against: their typology, roles, ideologies, behavior and relations with the rank and file of the groups concerned.

Policies and measures. The aim, in this part of the study, will be, after having acquired an objective understanding of the structure of the multiracial society, its functioning and basic trends, to analyze, on that basis, the role played by the policies to combat racial discrimination.

Legislative and other prescriptive measures (conventions, regulations, decrees, etc.). This part of each national study, should include a detailed and careful analytical description of the lines along which the policies and measures have developed in the society; the causes and motivations of the actions taken; the personnel, machinery, sponsorship, organization, functioning and other institutional aspects of the apparatus; its sporadic or continuous character; and the events, pressures and groups involved in the decisions to apply the policies and measures.

For the purpose of the analysis, a complete survey will be made, aiming at a systematic presentation of the antidiscriminatory measures taken in each society.

For each prescriptive measure, we must know:

(a) *nature and source*—for instance, law of Parliament, decree, court decision, agreement between parties, etc., date (year and month);
(b) *stated objective and brief background* of reasons for measure;
(c) *basic norms prescribed*—general rules and requirements prescribed;
(d) *sanctions*—kinds of sanctions and conditions of application;
(e) *when, how and who may invoke*—for example, the victims themselves, public authorities, attorneys, other parties, etc., being a detailed description of the actual functioning of the machinery established;
(f) *application and enforcement*—application of the prescriptive measures in

typical concrete situations, including whether and how the application of the norms and jurisprudence has changed, been adapted or altered from its original purposes;

(g) *appraisal*—who assesses and reviews the results of the policies applied; if such an appraisal exists, its functioning must be described;

(h) *other comments*—other pertinent observations not made explicit in the above list.

A careful analysis must be made of the role of the government as a whole, as well as of its various branches—especially the police machinery, the law and the courts—in the patterns of racial relations and in their changing trends.

It is important to make clear that this will not be repetition of what is said in the laws and documents, but clarification and explanation of any discrepancy that may exist between the law on the books and its enforcement. Court decisions and/or other significant encounters between principles and practices must be carefully examined. It will be appropriate to attach to each study documentation concerning the basic legislation and jurisprudence on the matter.

Another aspect deserving special attention is that of the policies of forced assimilation that not infrequently provoke contraassimilation reactions from the groups involved. The same applies to the policies enforcing—or prohibiting—discrimination in taxation, housing, schools, "job reservation," quota systems, etc. These must be analyzed from the point of view of the ideal models they offer, the implementation they receive, and the real targets they reach.

Preventive legislation, in terms for instance, of making unlawful the propagation of racist values and ideas, must be considered in all aspects, especially in its application to concrete situations.

In some countries, especially the newly independent ones, the process of acquiring, changing or losing citizenship and nationality, as well as the rules concerning the right of some groups to preserve traditions, customs, folkways, religion, education, language and symbols, express philosophy concerning the problems of assimilation and/or segregation, and must be the subject of special consideration in the study. Legislation concerning "job reservation," right of association, marriage and education are some examples of special fields to be considered.

With regard to the effectiveness of the role of law as a tool against discrimination, there may be evidence that other social processes must occur in order to provide the prerequisites of law enforcement. It has already been suggested, for example, that legal measures against discrimination increase in effectiveness when other factors in a society multiply the number of individuals ready to adjust their overt behavior to the prevailing legal rules, independent of any evaluation of content according to the principle *dura lex sed lex*. In other words, various social factors may increase the number of individuals whose basic orientation will be to obey the law—whether discriminatory or antidiscriminatory. There may be an increase in the number of "prejudiced-but-non-discriminators," whose characteristics fit the profile of the so-called "authoritarian personality" (Adorno), this being apparent in societies in which there is a trend toward centralization of power. Using this as a working hypothesis, and applying it to the society under study, new aspects of the problem may be discovered.

Considering that some social groups have a strategic role in dealing with members of other ethnic groups and in spreading their own attitudes, it is important to analyze the measures from the point of view of the special groups they have as targets: youth, teachers, workers, military, civil servants, clergymen, physicians, lawyers.

Measures of persuasion and promotion. For our research purposes, they would be provisionally classified as follows:

(a) *Exhortation*—appeals, speeches, statements, recommendations, etc. Who makes them? Why? For what specific purposes? When? Case studies of the most typical cases will be made and whenever possible, original documentation will be attached to the reports.

(b) *Education*—meaning the formal and systematic use of the educational apparatus as a tool against racial conflict, prejudice and discrimination. Content analysis of syllabi, textbooks; interviews with students, teachers, parents, are recommended approaches to obtain insight into this aspect of the problem. The analysis must pay special attention to the secondary or high school level, because of its strategic importance in conditioning racial attitudes.

(c) *Information*—as circulated to the general public through mass media of communication. Its role in the formation and/or transformation of racial feelings will be analyzed here, emphasizing not only the effects of the intentional use of these media for the purpose but also the patterns on awareness revealed, remembering that it is easier to create than to eliminate racial attitudes.

(d) *Participation*—in multiracial associations and/or activities, guided by the idea that keeping in touch and acting together leads to increasing reduction of racial tensions. Case studies of most typical attempts made together with the effects will be undertaken.

(e) *Negotiation*—as a pattern of solving open conflicts between ethnic groups— established by law, tradition, or by agreement between interested parties. This approach has been experimented with in different fields (trade unions, employment, urban settlements, schools, etc.), especially when the groups concerned have reached a high level or organization along racial lines.

(f) *Treatment*—meaning a clinical approach with explicit therapeutical goals. After the Second World War, this approach came into vogue in many countries, and its use, abuse and real effects will be analyzed in the society under study.

These categories are not intended to be exhaustive, and others may be added according to the particular experience of each society concerned.

Actions and reactions of the groups. The actions and reactions of the groups involved, their ideologies and degrees of organization, patterns of leadership and of active participation in the combat against racial discrimination will be another aspect of the problem deserving special consideration. Such consideration will be given systematically, carefully taking into account the characteristics of each society under study.

Successes and failures. In the final part of each study, the interpretation and evaluation of the existing trends, as revealed by the study as a whole, will be made explicit. This interpretation and evaluation of the policies and measures taken since World War II to combat racial discrimination, as well as of their effectiveness, may provide answers to the three basic questions: (a) In what direction are the patterns of racial relations changing? (b) What has been the role played by the measures taken and the policies applied? (c) What has been the role played by spontaneous, nondeliberate factors, connected with the dynamics of the racial situation itself, as factors of change?

Where necessary, a clear indication should be given, stating whether or not the opinions expressed coincide with the points of view prevailing in (a) local "public opinion"; (b) the governing circles of the society under study; and/or (c) the different groups involved.

The assessment of the successes and failures of the policies applied, to be done intelligently, must recognize that nobody expects any "measure" taken in isolation to solve any racial problem of any society. Also, from this point of view, no measure could be completely "effective" in the sense that its absence or lack of application would be the main factor responsible for the existence, or for the continuation, of the racial problem.

Racial discrimination is an extremely complex problem; its typology is manifold. Easy formulas or specific "measures" to solve other social problems—war, prostitution, poverty, neurosis, drug addiction, delinquency, illiteracy—do not exist, and the same applies to racial discrimination.

We must, therefore, approach the "measures" and "remedies" attempted as a whole, as forming a pattern of prevailing and developing racial policy in the society concerned. The analysis of each "measure" *per se* is conceived of as a step leading to the understanding of the racial policy in the total breadth and complexity of its meaning.

In evaluating the successes and failures of the policies applied as well as of their effects, some strategic questions must be raised, and used as basic working hypotheses to be checked by direct observation of the situation under study and by the systematic analysis and interpretation of the documentation collected in the fieldwork.

Some examples of those strategic questions to which the study must offer scholarly and well-documented answers, are given below. It must, however, be made clear that criteria for measuring the effectiveness of the measures and policies should be refined in the light of further study and discussion with those who will participate in the study.

In many cases, the techniques most frequently used are not the most pertinent—being preferred more for their latent functions than for the manifest one (i.e., imitation, less costly, discharge or guilt complexes, etc.). From this point of view, what is the case with the situations under study?

There commonly exists a gap between scientific knowledge regarding the processes of racial relations and the underlying philosophy of the antidiscriminatory practices and measures. What is the situation in the societies under study? At which stage, or level, does theoretical knowledge form the basis of practical measures?

Failure of measures applied tends to increase frustration and unrest. Sometimes, the mere announcement of a "measure" to be taken is considered as a satisfactory step against discrimination, thus relying on the efficacy of a "moral warning." It is also assumed by some that the mere passage of the law probably decreases the incidence of discrimination. What, from this point of view, is the situation in the society under study?

One of the most typical heritages of some domination patterns of the past—for instance, the colonial system—is the fact that the subordinate groups continue for a long time to look at themselves through the eyes of the dominating groups, accepting the negative image about themselves. Is the eradication of these self-depreciating views one of the goals of the antidiscriminatory policies? To what extent is this made explicit? What are the measures and techniques specifically used for this purpose? What are the results obtained?

"Discretion is the best policy"—"It is not wise to publicize racial tensions." How far is this found in the societies under study? With what results? If changes have occurred, what were the reasons and under what pressures?

An intensification of intergroup tensions and discriminatory practices may, in many cases, be the result of the fact that some basic problems are being solved, that the groups are moving in social space, that a process of structural change is going on, stimulating the rise in discrimination as a compensatory and stabilizing factor. How far, and why, does this model fit, or not fit, each society under study? To what extent do the policies applied take this into consideration?

Some policies put the emphasis on changing the status of those discriminated against in order to improve their situation and image; other policies emphasize changing the attitudes of the discriminators. From this point of view, what is the prevailing pattern in the society under study? Why was it preferred?

Social and economic policies, applied for other purposes, not explicitly to combat racial discrimination, may have an impact on the racial problem. What have these measures been and what has been their impact? Here, special consideration must be given to policies of agrarian reform, antipoverty programs, popular education, technical training, community development, etc.

The "prejudiced outlook" and its institutional framework forms a relatively integrated unit. How far and in what ways do the policies applied take this into account? In practice, what is the corresponding integration of policies applied to combat various discrimination: religious, national, linguistic, against women, against foreigners, against handicapped people, etc.?

Policies aiming to remove the structural factors of racial discrimination usually raise resistance on the part of those with vested interests in these social cleavages. In each society concerned—Who are those with vested interests? Why do they oppose changes? How is this expressed in practice? To what extent, and how, do the policies applied take this into account?

Special consideration is also to be given to international aspects. In the modern world, international implications of national racial problems are of the utmost importance. Two main directions are: (a) the national "race" problem becoming an international issue; (b) trends in world politics deeply influencing, for better or for worse, the evolution of the national racial situation. These international implications must be approached from different points of view as for instance: Migration to other countries of groups discriminated against; solidarity or support for resistance movements received from aborad; existing "spreading factors" in other countries that could be affected by developments in the situation of the nation considered; connections of the racial problem with tribal, national or other patterns of solidarity or conflict involving more than one nation, etc. Last, but not least, the presence and influence of the efforts of the United Nations in combating racial discrimination and in defending human rights will be considered, with special emphasis on the identification of weak points and suggestions for better performance in the future.

Comparing the policies applied, as factors of change, with the spontaneous factors connected with the dynamics of the racial situation itself—as has already been indicated—is another basic aim of the evaluation to be undertaken. The explicit aim here is to understand what is happening in the various relevant sectors of the social, economic and political structure that are changing (indicating in what direction and with what intensity) the institutional framework within which the groups enter into relations with each other, the systems of social roles they perform and the orientations and effectiveness of the policies applied. Thus, what seems to be important is the notion that antidiscriminatory policies operate in a context in which everything else does not remain equal and that other factors are present and influential in the changing configuration of the racial situation. This analysis would also be based on the fact that the effectiveness of measures against racial discrimination is largely dependent upon the patterns and degrees of correlation between "racial" and "nonracial" processes, "deliberate" and "nondeliberate" factors, and "ethnic" and "nonethnic" trends.

Difficulties and Obstacles for the Study

In proposing such studies and providing a research design for information, UNITAR is aware of the many difficulties and obstacles. First of all, there is always a certain amount of sensitivity on the part of authorities to admit the existence of problems of race relations. This results in resistance to any study in depth on the situation prevailing in a particular society. This has also prevented the adoption of concrete antidiscriminatory measures and where adopted, the implementing machinery is often subsumed in other forms of social welfare activities and where the law is ambiguous the problems of enforcement are considerable. Proportionately the task of evaluation is made more difficult. In many societies, most people who suffer the humiliation of being discriminated against prefer to forget it or suffer the affront in silence. They are also afraid of creating a situation in which their complaints would lead to more organized discrimination. This being the case it will be exceedingly difficult for individuals or institutions to collect evidence more or less accurately as to the extent of discrimination and forms which it takes. While sample surveys are useful methods of discovering the extent of racial discrimination, through interviews, situation testing etc., one should not underestimate the problems involved in it. First of all, these are expensive undertakings. An important requisite for the reliability and relevance of the sample surveys is the confidence created by the investigators in both the discriminators and the discriminated and the cooperation received from different sections of the community as well as the administrative units at local, regional and national levels.

The second hurdle to be faced is in relation to statistical data of every kind. Although basic demographic data are being gradually compiled on a systematic basis in a number of countries, there is a reluctance to keep statistics that distinguish by race or ethnic group. In fact, the attempts at removing racial distinctions as a part of antidiscriminatory measures have obliterated the statistical data necessary for the study. This difficulty in the collection of figures will be more compounded when we move into the area of education, housing, employment and financial sectors involving mortgages, insurance and credit facilities. But since the main purpose is evaluation of the effectiveness of measures against racial discrimination, the difficulties encountered in data collection should not deter the prosecution of the study.

The enumeration of some of these difficulties is made not to discourage the undertaking of these studies. On the contrary, the challenges involved should spur greater efforts and the beneficial results would be, not only in the field of racial discrimination, but also in other sectors of public life, associated with this problem.

Bibliography

Books

Ackerman, Nathan and Johoda, Marie, *Anti-Semitism and Emotional Disorder* New York: Harper and Row, 1950.

Adorno, T.W., et al., *The Authoritarian Personality*. New York: Harper and Row, 1950.

Banton, Michael, *Race Relations*. New York: Basic Books, Inc., 1967.

Bettelheim, Bruno and Janowitz, Morris, *Dynamics of Prejudice: A Psychological and Sociological Study of Veterans*. New York: Harper and Row, 1950.

Blood, Robert O. Jr., *Northern Breakthrough*. California: Wadsworth Publishing Co., Inc., 1968.

Brink, William and Harris, Louis, *The Negro Revolution in America*. New York: Simon and Schuster, 1964.

Davidson, Basil, *The African Slave Trade*. Boston: Little, Brown and Co., 1961.

Dean, John P. and Rosen, Alex, *A Manual of Intergroup Relations*. Chicago: University of Chicago Press, 1955.

Denton, John H. *Apartheid American Style*. Berkeley, California: Diablo Press, 1967.

Dewey, John, *Intelligence in the Modern World*. New York: Modern Library, Random House, 1939.

Dollard, John, *Caste and Class in a Southern Town*. Garden City, New York: Doubleday Anchor Books, 1957.

Eley, Lynn W. and Casterens, Thomas W., *The Politics of Fair-Housing Legislation: State and Local Case Studies*. San Francisco: Chandler Publishing Co., 1968.

Elkins, Stanley M., *Slavery: A Problem in American Institutional and Intellectual Life*. Chicago: University of Chicago Press, 1959.

Gamson, William, *Power and Discontent*. Homewood, Illinois: Dorsey Press, 1968.

Glazer, Nathan and McEntire, Davis, *Studies in Housing and Minority Groups*. Berkeley: University of California Press, 1960.

Greenberg, Jack, *Race Relations and American Law*. New York: Columbia University Press, 1959.

Grier, George and Grier, Eunice, *Equality and Beyond: Housing Segregation and the Goals of the Great Society*. Chicago: Quadrangle Books, 1966.

Helper, Rose, *Racial Policies and Practices of Real Estate Brokers*. Minneapolis: University of Minnesota Press, 1969.

Hiestrand, Dale L., *Economic Growth and Employment Opportunities for Minorities*. New York: Columbia University Press, 1964.

International Labor Office. *Fighting Discrimination in Employment and Occupation*. Geneva: International Labour Office, 1968.

Johnson, Charles S., *Patterns of Negro Segregation*. New York: Harper and Brothers, 1943.

Killian, Lewis M., *White Southerners*. New York: Random House, 1970.

Lee, Frank F., *Negro and White in Connecticut Town*. New Haven, Connecticut: College and University Press, 1961.

Litwach, Leon F., *North of Slavery*. Chicago: Phoenix Books, University of Chicago Press, 1961.

Marshall, Ray, *The Negro Worker*. New York: Random House, 1967.

McEntire, David, *Residence and Race*. Berkeley: University of California Press, 1960.

Mendelson, Wallace, *Discrimination*. Englewood Cliffs, New Jersey: Prentice-Hall, Inc., 1962.

Miller, S.M., and Riessman, Frank, *Social Class and Social Policy*. New York: Basic Books, 1968.

Moynihan, Daniel P., *Maximum Feasible Misunderstanding*. New York: Free Press, 1969.

Murphy, Raymond J. and Elinson, Howard, *Problems and Prospects of the Negro Movement*. Belmont, California: Wadsworth Publishing Co., 1968.

Myrdal, Gunnar, *An American Dilemma*. New York: Harper and Brothers, 1957.

National Advisory Commission, *Report of the National Advisory Commission on Civil Disorder*. New York: Bantam Books, 1966.

Norgren, Paul H., "Fair Employment Practice Laws—Experience, Effects, Prospects," in *Employment, Race, and Poverty*, edited by Arthur M. Ross and Herbert Hill. New York: Harcourt, Brace and World, 1967.

Orfield, Gary, *The Reconstruction of Southern Education*. New York: Wiley Interscience, 1969.

Parkes, James W., *An Enemy of the People: Anti-Semitism*. Penguin, 1946.

Pinckny, Alphonso, *Black Americans*. Englewood Cliffs, New Jersey: Prentice-Hall, Inc., 1969.

Price, James L., *Organizational Effectiveness*. Homewood, Illinois: Richard D. Irwin, Inc., 1968.

Quarles, Benjamin, *The Negro in the Making of America*. New York: Collier Books, Macmillan, 1964.

Rokeach, Milton, *The Open and Closed Mind*. New York: Basic Books, Inc., 1960.

Simpson, George Eaton and Yinger, J. Milton, *Racial and Cultural Minorities*. New York: Harper and Row, 1965.

Sovern, Michael, *Legal Restraints on Racial Discrimination in Employment*. New York: Twentieth Century Fund, 1966.

125

Spear, Allan H., *Black Chicago, The Making of a Negro Ghetto 1890-1920*. Chicago: University of Chicago Press, 1967.

Stampp, Kenneth M., *The Peculiar Institution: Slavery in the Ante-Bellum South*. New York: Vintage Books, Random House, 1956.

Stone, Chuck, *Black Political Power in America*. New York: Bobbs-Merrill Co., 1968.

Taeuber, Karl and Alma, *Negroes in Cities*. Chicago: Aldine Publishing Co., 1965.

U.S. Commission on Civil Rights, *Civil Rights*. Washington, D.C.: U.S. Government Printing Office, 1963.

U.S. Commission on Civil Rights, *Civil Rights Digest*. Washington, D.C.: U.S. Government Printing Office, 1964.

U.S. Commission on Civil Rights, *Education*. Washington, D.C.: U.S. Government Printing Office, Book 2, 1961.

U.S. Commission on Civil Rights, Federal Civil Rights Enforcement Efforts. Washington, D.C.: U.S. Government Printing Office, 1970.

U.S. Commission on Civil Rights, *Political Participation*. Washington, D.C.: U.S. Government Printing Office, 1968.

U.S. Commission on Civil Rights, *Racial Isolation in the Public Schools*. Washington, D.C.: U.S. Government Printing Office, 1967.

Van den Berghe, Pierre, *Race and Racism: A Comparative Perspective*. New York: John Wiley and Sons, 1967.

Vander Zanden, James W., *American Minority Relations*. New York: Ronald Press Co., 1963.

Vander Zanden, James W., *Race Relations in Transition: The Segregation Crisis Within the South*. New York: Random House, Inc., 1965.

Williams, Robin, *Strangers Next Door*. Englewood Cliffs, New Jersey: Prentice-Hall, 1964.

Woodward, C. Vann, *The Strange Career of Jim Crow*. New York: Oxford University Press, 1966.

Zilversmit, Arthur, *The First Emancipation: The Abolition of Slavery in the North*. Chicago: University of Chicago Press, 1967.

Articles

Baron, Harold M., et al., "Black Powerlessness in Chicago," *Trans-Action*, 1968.

Barron, Milton L., "A Content Analysis of Intergroup Humor," *American Sociological Review*, 15, 1950.

Becker, Howard S., and Horowitz, Irving Louis, "The Culture of Civility," *Trans-Action*, April, 1970.

Blake, Robert and Dennis, Wayne, "The Development of Stereotypes Concerning the Negro," *Journal of Abnormal and Social Psychology*, 38, 1943.

Brink, William and Harris, Louis, "What Whites Think of Negroes," in *Problems and Prospects of the Negro Movement*. Belmont, California: Wadsworth Publishing Co., 1968.

Broom, Leonard and Glenn, Norval D., "The Occupations and Income of Black Americans," in *Blacks in the United States*, edited by Norval D. Glenn and Charles M. Bonjean. San Francisco: Chandler Publishing Co., 1969.

Broom, Leonard and Glenn, Norval D., "When Will America's Negroes Catch Up?" *Power and the Black Community*, edited by Sethard Fisher, New York: Random House, 1970.

Byrne, Donn and Wong, Terry, "Interpersonal Attraction and Assumed Dissimilarity of Attitudes," *Journal of Abnormal and Social Psychology*, October, 1962.

Campbell, A. and Schuman, H., "Black Views of Racial Issues," in *Black Americans and White Racism*. New York: Holt, Rinehart, and Winston, 1970.

Campbell, A., and Schuman, H., "White Beliefs about Negroes," in *Black Americans and White Racism*. New York: Holt, Rinehart, and Winston, 1970.

Cartwright, Walter J. and Burtis, Thomas R., "Race and Intelligence: Changing Opinions in Social Science," in *Blacks in the United States*, edited by Norval D. Glenn and Charles M. Bonjean. San Francisco: Chandler Publishing Co., 1969.

Coleman, James S., "Race Relations and Social Change," in *Race and the Social Sciences*, edited by Irwin Katz and Patricia Gurin. New York: Basic Books, Inc., 1969.

Feshbach, Seymour and Singer, Robert, "The Effects of Personal and Shared Threats Upon Social Prejudice," *Journal of Abnormal and Social Psychology*, 1957.

Gilbert, Neil and Eaton, Joseph W., "Favoritism as a Strategy in Race Relations," *Social Problems*. Summer, 1970.

Glaser, Daniel, "The Sentiments of Soldiers Abroad Toward Europeans," *American Journal of Sociology*, 1946.

Glenn, Norval D., "Changes in Social and Economic Conditions of Black Americans during the 1960's," in *Blacks in the United States*, edited by Norval D. Glenn and Charles M. Bonjean. San Francisco: Chandler Publishing Co., 1969.

Glenn, Norval D., "The Role of White Resistance and Facilitation in the Negro Struggle for Equality," in *Power and the Black Community*. edited by Sethard Fisher. New York: Random House, 1970.

Glenn, Norval D., "White Gains from Negro Subordination," *Black in the United States*, edited by Norval D. Glenn and Charles M. Bonjean. San Francisco: Chandler Publishing Co., 1969.

Glickstein, Howard A., "Statement, Staff Director-Designate, U.S. Commission on Civil Rights, Before the Senate Subcommittee on Labor of the Committee on Labor and Public Welfare," U.S. Civil Rights Commission, September 10, 1969.

Goodman, Mary E., *Race Awareness in Young Children*. Cambridge: Addison-Wesley, 1952.

Hamblin, Robert J., "The Dynamics of Racial Discrimination," *Social Problems*. 1962.

Hannah, John A., Chairman of the U.S. Civil Rights Commission, *Letters* To George P. Shultz, Secretary of Labor, February 4, 1969.

Hill, Herbert, "The Racial Practice of Organized Labor—The Age of Gompers and After," in *Employment, Race, and Poverty*, edited by Arthur M. Ross and Herbert Hill. New York: Harcourt, Brace and World, Inc., 1967.

Horowitz, Eugene L. and Ruth E., "Development of Social Attitudes in Children," *Sociometry*, 1, 1938.

Hutchinson, John E., "The AFL-CIO and the Negro" in *Employment, Race, and Poverty*, edited by Arthur M. Ross and Herbert Hill. New York: Harcourt, Brace and World, 1967.

Izard, C.E., "Personality Similarity and Friendship," *American Psychologist*, 1959.

Krislov, Samuel, "Government and Equal Employment Opportunity," in *Employment, Race and Poverty*, edited by Arthur M. Ross and Herbert Hill. New York: Harcourt, Brace and World, 1967.

LeMelle, Tilden J., "Public Policy and Anti-Black Discrimination in the United States," in *Report on the International Research Conference on Race Relations*. Center on International Race Relations, University of Denver, 1970.

Lott, A.J., and Rosell, J., "Race, Sex, and Assumed Similarity," *American Psychologist*, 1959.

Matthews, Donald R., "Political Science Research on Race Relations," in *Race and the Social Sciences*, edited by Irwin Katz and Patricia Gurin. New York: Basic Books, 1969.

Matthews, Donald R. and Prothro, James W., "Political Factors and Negro Voter Registration in the South," *American Political Science Review*, Vol. 57, No. 2, 1963.

McCord, William, McCord, Joan and Howard, Alan, "Early Familial Experiences and Bigotry," *American Sociological Review*, 1960.

Meier, August, "Civil Rights Strategies for Negro Employment," in *Employment, Race and Poverty*, edited by Arthur M. Ross and Herbert Hill. New York: Harcourt, Brace and World, 1967.

Moreland, Kenneth J., "Racial Recognition by Nursery School Children in Lynchburg, Virginia," *Social Forces*, 1958.

128

Moskos, Charles C. Jr., "Racial Integration in the Armed Forces," in *Blacks in the United States*, edited by Norval D. Glenn and Charles M. Bonjean. San Francisco: Chandler Publishing Co., 1969.

Norgren, Paul H., "Fair Employment Practice Laws—Experience, Effects, Prospects," in *Employment, Race and Poverty*, edited by Arthur M. Ross and Herbert Hill. New York: Harcourt, Brace and World, 1967.

Northrup, Herbert R., "Industry's Racial Employment Policies," in *Employment, Race and Poverty*, edited by Arthur M. Ross and Herbert Hill. New York: Harcourt, Brace and World, 1967.

Pearlin, Leonard I., "Shifting Group Attachments and Attitudes Toward Negroes," *Social Forces*, 33, 1954.

Pepitone, Albert and Wallace, W., "Experimental Studies on the Dynamics of Hostility." Paper read at Pennsylvania Psychological Assoc. Meetings, 1955. (Described in Albert Pepitone, "Attributions of Causality, Social Attitudes, and Cognitive Matching Processes," in *Person Perception and Interpersonal Behavior*, edited by Renato Tagiuri and Luigi Petrullo, Stanford: Stanford University Press, 1958.

Quinn, Olive W., "The Transmission of Racial Attitudes Among Southerners," *Social Forces*, 33, 1954.

Roberts, A.H. and Rokeach, Milton, "Anomie, Authoritarianism and Prejudice: A Replication," *American Journal of Sociology*, January, 1956.

Rose, Arnold, *The Roots of Prejudice*. (UNESCO), 1961.

Rosenfled, H. and Jackson, J., "Effect of Similarity of Personalities on Interpersonal Attraction," *American Psychologist*, 14, 1959.

Ross, Michael J., Crawford, Thomas, and Pettigrew, Thomas, "Negro-Neighbors-Banned in Boston," *Trans-Action*, 3, No. 6, 1966.

Schuman, Howard, "Sociological Racism," *Trans-Action*, Vol. 7, No. 2, December, 1969.

Sheppard, Harold L., "The Negro-Merchant: A Study of Negro Anti-Semitism," *American Journal of Sociology*, 53, 1957.

Sherif, Muzafer, "Experiments in Group Conflict," *Scientific American*, 195, 1956.

Shuval, Judith T., "Emerging Patterns of Ethnic Strain in Israel," *Social Forces*, 40, 1962.

Tauber, Karl E., "Residential Segregation," *Scientific American*. August, 1965.

Thompson, Robert A., Lewis, Hylan, and McEntire, Davis, "Atlanta and Birmingham A Comparative Study in Negro Housing," in *Studies in Housing and Minority Groups*, edited by Nathan Glazer and Davis McEntire. Berkeley: University of California Press, 1960.

Orne, Martin T. and Evans, Frederick J., "Social Control in the Psychological Experiment," *Journal of Personality and Social Psychology*, 1, 1965.

U.S. Commission on Civil Rights, "Evaluation of Title VI of Civil Rights Act of 1964, U.S. Department of Agriculture," July, 1968.

U.S. Commission on Civil Rights, "Federal Enforcement of School Desegregation," September 11, 1969.

U.S. Commission on Civil Rights, memo dealing with discrimination in state and local governments, November 6, 1968.

U.S. Department of Commerce, "Selected Characteristics of Persons and Families," *Population Characteristics*, Bureau of Census Series P-20, No. 189, August 18, 1969.

U.S. Department of Labor, Bureau of Labor Statistics, *The Negroes in the United States: Their Economic and Social Situation*, Bulletin No. 1511, 1966.

Westie, Frank R. and Howard, David H., "Social Status Differentials and the Race Attitudes of Negroes," *American Sociological Review*, 19, 1954.

Westie, Frank R., "The American Dilemma: An Empirical Test," in *Blacks in the United States*, edited by Norval D. Glenn and Charles M. Bonjean. Reprinted from the *American Sociological Review*, 30, August, 1965.

Notes

Chapter 1
Discrimination and Racial Relations:
A Theoretical Perspective

1. James W. Vander Zanden, *American Minority Relations* (New York: Ronald Press Co., 1963), pp. 8-9.

2. Michael Banton, *Race Relations* (New York: Basic Books, Inc., 1967), p. 8.

3. *Fighting Discrimination in Employment and Occupation* (Geneva: International Labour Office, 1968), p. 7.

4. Donald R. Matthews and James W. Prothro, "Political Factors and Negro Voter Registration in the South," *American Political Science Review*, Vol. 57, No. 2, June, 1963, p. 366.

5. Banton, *Race Relations*, p. 140.

6. Herbert Hill, "The Racial Practice of Organized Labor," in *The Negro and the American Labor Movement*, edited by Julius Jacobson, (Garden City, New York: Doubleday, 1968), pp. 297-298.

7. Frank F. Lee, *Negro and White in Connecticut Town* (New Haven, Connecticut: College and University Press, 1961), p. 94.

8. James W. Vander Zanden, *Race Relations in Transition* (New York: Random House, 1967), p. 35.

9. Tamotsu Shibutani and Kian Kwan, *Ethnic Stratification: A Comparative Approach* (New York: Macmillan Co., 1965), p. 40.

10. The most confused of these works is the recent *Institutional Racism in America* by Louis L. Knowles and Kenneth Prewitt (Englewood Cliffs, New Jersey: Prentice-Hall, 1969).

Chapter 2
Historical Summary of Black Discrimination and
Black-White Stratification in the United States

1. Basil Davidson, *The African Slave Trade* (Boston: Little, Brown and Co., 1961), pp. 45-51, 80-87, 102-107; Benjamin Quarles, *The Negro in the Making of America* (N.Y.: Collier Books, Macmillan, 1964), pp. 19-23.

2. Quarles, *The Negro*, pp. 33-37; Stanley M. Elkins, *Slavery: A Problem in American Institutional and Intellectual Life* (Chicago: University of Chicago Press, 1959), pp. 38-39; Kenneth M. Stampp, *The Peculiar Institution: Slavery in*

the Ante-Bellum South (New York: Vintage Books, Random House, 1956), pp. 21-22.

3. Stampp, *Peculiar Institution*, pp. 22-23. Elkins, op. cit., p. 40.

4. Kenneth M. Stampp, *The Peculiar Institution: Slavery in the Ante-Bellum South* (N.Y.: Vintage Books, Random House, 1956). Stanley Elkins, *Slavery: A Problem in American Institutional and Intellectual Life* (N.Y.: Harper and Row, 1959).

5. Stampp, *Peculiar Institution*, pp. 150, 252; Elkins, op. cit., pp. 54-55.

6. Stampp, *Peculiar Institution*, pp. 149, 209.

7. Stampp, *Peculiar Institution*, pp. 150, 197, 208; Elkins, op. cit., p. 59.

8. Stampp, *Peculiar Institution*, pp. 207-209.

9. Ibid.

10. Stampp, *Peculiar Institution*, p. 208; Elkins, op. cit., pp. 60-61.

11. Stampp, *Peculiar Institution*, p. 208.

12. Ibid., pp. 197-8, 222-277.

13. Elkins, *Slavery*, pp. 98-133.

14. Stampp, *Peculiar Institution*, p. 148.

15. Elkins, *Slavery*, pp. 130-131.

16. Stampp, *Peculiar Institution*, pp. 151, 154, 172-3, 210-214.

17. Ibid., pp. 164-169.

18. Several excellent books have extensively treated the subject of racism. The most notable are: William Stanton, *The Leopard's Spots: Scientific Attitudes Toward Race in America, 1815-1850* (Chicago: University of Chicago Press, 1960). Thomas F. Gossett, *Race: The History of an Idea in America* (Dallas: Southern Methodist University Press, 1963. Winthrop D. Jordan, *White Over Black—American Attitudes Toward the Negro—1550-1812* (Williamsburg, Va.: University of No. Carolina Press, 1968). David Brion Davis, *The Problem of Slavery in Western Culture* (Ithaca: Cornell University Press, 1966).

19. *Southern Literary Messenger*, 1835.

20. Leon F. Litwack, *North of Slavery* (Chicago: Phoenix Books, University of Chicago Press, 1961), pp. 66, 70-74. Arthur Zilversmit, *The First Emancipation: The Abolition of Slavery in the North* (Chicago: Univ. of Chicago Press, 1967), pp. 12-13.

21. Litwack, *North*, p. 66.

22. Litwack, *North*, pp. 93-94; Zilversmit, op. cit., pp. 14-15, 21.

23. Ibid., p. 93.

24. Litwack, *North*, pp. 31-33, 61-62, 79-82.

25. Ibid., p. 62.

26. Ibid., p. 79.

27. Ibid., pp. 31-33.

28. Zilversmit, *Emancipation*, pp. 12-13.

29. Litwack, *North*, p. 93; Zilversmit, *Emancipation*, pp. 16-19.

30. Litwack, *North*, pp. 114-115, 132-135.

31. Ibid., pp. 114-115.

32. Ibid., pp. 97, 196.

33. C. Vann Woodward, *The Strange Career of Jim Crow* (New York: Oxford University Press, 1966), pp. 18-19.

34. Ibid., pp. 44-82.

35. Ibid., p. 25.

36. Ibid., p. 33.

37. Charles S. Johnson, *Patterns of Negro Segregation* (New York: Harper and Brothers, 1943), p. 83.

38. Woodward, *Strange Career*, p. 29.

39. Banton, *Relations*, p. 140.

40. Johnson, *Patterns*, p. 84.

41. Woodward, *Strange Career*, p. 85.

42. Banton, *Relations*, p. 141.

43. Pierre L. van den Berghe, *Race and Racism: A Comparative Perspective* (New York: John Wiley and Sons, 1967), pp. 89-90.

44. Gunnar Myrdal, *An American Dilemma* (New York: Harper and Brothers, 1944), pp. 282, 287, 304, 323, 325, 380; Johnson, *Patterns*, pp. 90-99.

45. Myrdal, *Dilemma*, p. 282.

46. Johnson, *Patterns*, p. 97.

47. Ibid., pp. 98-99.

48. Myrdal, *Dilemma*, pp. 319-20, 339-342, 897; Johnson, *Patterns*, pp. 12-19; Dollard *Caste*, pp. 191-2, 196.

49. Johnson, *Patterns*, p. 13.

50. Myrdal, *Dilemma*, p. 339.

51. Johnson, *Patterns*, pp. 18-19.

52. Myrdal, *Dilemma*, pp. 482-486; Dollard, *Caste*, p. 209.

53. Myrdal, *Dilemma*, p. 482.

54. Ibid., p. 484.

55. Dollard, *Caste*, p. 209.

56. Myrdal, *Dilemma*, pp. 535, 549-551; Johnson, *Patterns*, pp. 30, 33, 35.

57. Myrdal, *Dilemma*, pp. 346-7, 634-635; Johnson, *Patterns*, pp. 27-29, 44-52, 56-57, 65-66, 72; Dollard, *Caste*, pp. 352-3.

58. Johnson, *Patterns*, p. 29.

59. Myrdal, *Dilemma*, p. 347.

60. Myrdal, *Dilemma*, pp. 607, 613; Johnson, *Patterns*, pp. 59, 76, 125, 128, 136, 143, 147-8; Dollard, *Caste*, pp. 184-5, 351-2.

61. Johnson, *Patterns*, p. 77.

62. Myrdal, *Dilemma*, p. 639.

63. Davis McEntire, *Residence and Race* (Berkeley: University of California Press, 1960), p. 258. Nathan Glazer and Davis McEntire, *Studies in Housing and Minority Groups*. (Berkeley: University of California Press, 1960), p. 59.

64. George Grier and Eunice Grier, *Equality and Beyond: Housing Segregation and the Goals of the Great Society* (Chicago: Quadrangle Books, 1966), p. 54.

65. Dollard, *Caste*, p. 117.

66. Allan H. Spear, *Black Chicago, The Making of a Negro Ghetto 1890-1920* (Chicago: University of Chicago Press, 1967).

67. Ibid., pp. 5-7.

68. Alphonso Pinckny, *Black Americans* (Englewood Cliffs, New Jersey: Prentice-Hall, Inc., 1969), p. 47-49; Spear, *Chicago*, p. 12.

69. Spear, *Chicago*, pp. 21-25.

70. Spear, *Chicago*, pp. 34, 159; Myrdal, *Dilemma*, pp. 304-306, 323, 326; Herbert Hill, "The Racial Practice of Organized Labor—The Age of Gompers and After," in *Employment, Race, and Poverty*, edited by Arthur M. Ross and Herbert Hill (New York: Harcourt, Brace & World, Inc., 1967), pp. 391-392.

71. Hill, *Labor*, p. 391.

72. Ibid., p. 392.

73. Myrdal, *Dilemma*, p. 306.

74. Spear, *Chicago*, p. 227; Myrdal, *Dilemma*, p. 308.

75. Spear, *Chicago*, pp. 42, 116; Myrdal, *Dilemma*, pp. 346, 613.

76. Spear, *Chicago*, p. 44; Myrdal, *Dilemma*, p. 527.

77. Myrdal, *Dilemma*, p. 617.

78. Ibid., p. 635.

79. Ibid., p. 492.

80. Ibid., p. 528.

81. Ibid., p. 633.

82. Spear, *Chicago*, pp. 228-229.

Chapter 3
Changes in Racial Discrimination and Racial
Stratification since World War II

1. Leonard Broom and Norval D. Glenn, "The Occupations and Income of Black Americans," in *Blacks in the United States*, edited by Norval D. Glenn and Charles M. Bonjean (San Francisco: Chandler Publishing Co., 1969), p. 23.

2. Ibid., p. 24.

3. Ibid.

4. Ibid.

5. James W. Vander Zanden, *Race Relations in Transition: The Segregation Crisis Within the South* (N.Y.: Random House, Inc., 1965), pp. 15-16.

6. Ibid., p. 17.

7. *Report of the National Advisory Commission on Civil Disorder* (N.Y.: Bantam Books, 1966), pp. 239-240.

8. Ibid., p. 243.

9. Ibid.

10. James W. Vander Zanden, *Race Relations in Transition: The Segregation Crisis Within the South* (N.Y.: Random House, Inc., 1965), pp. 86-87.

11. Walter J. Cartwright and Thomas R. Burtis, "Race and Intelligence: Changing Opinions in Social Science," in *Blacks in the United States*, edited by Norval D. Glenn and Charles M. Bonjean (San Francisco: Chandler Publishing Co., 1969), p. 168.

12. See Howard Schuman, "Sociological Racism," *Trans-Action*, Vol. 7, No. 2, December, 1969, pp. 47-48. A. Campbell and H. Schuman, "White Beliefs About Negroes," in *Black Americans and White Racism*, edited by Marcel L. Goldschmid (N.Y.: Holt, Rinehart and Winston, Inc., 1970). William Brink and Louis Harris, *The Negro Revolution in America*, (N.Y.: Simon and Schuster, 1964).

13. Schuman, *Sociological*, pp. 47-48.

14. Tilden J. LeMelle, "Public Policy and Anti-Black Discrimination in the United States," in *Report on the International Research Conference on Race Relations* (Center on International Race Relations, University of Denver, 1970), pp. 132-143.

15. James S. Coleman, "Race Relations and Social Change," in *Race and the Social Sciences*, edited by Irwin Katz and Patricia Gurin (N.Y.: Basic Books, Inc., 1969), p. 278.

16. Neil Gilbert and Joseph W. Eaton, "Favoritism as a Strategy in Race Relations," *Social Problems*, Vol. 18, No. 1, Summer, 1970, p. 39.

17. Ibid.

18. Coleman, *Race Relations*, pp. 304-309.

19. U.S. Commission on Civil Rights, *Civil Rights Digest* (Washington, D.C.: U.S. Government Printing Office, August, 1964).

20. U.S. Commission on Civil Rights, *Federal Civil Rights Enforcement Effort* (Washington, D.C.: U.S. Government Printing Office, 1970), pp. 216-218.

21. Lynn W. Eley and Thomas W. Casstevens, *The Politics of Fair-Housing Legislation: State and Local Case Studies* (San Francisco: Chandler Publishing Co., 1968), pp. 4-5.

22. Ibid., pp. 5-6.

23. U.S. Commission on Civil Rights, *Civil Rights, 1963* (Washington, D.C.: U.S. Government Printing Office, 1963), pp. 96-97.

24. Ibid., p. 97.

25. Ibid., p. 98.

26. U.S. Commission on Civil Rights, *Federal Civil Rights Enforcement Effort* (Washington, D.C.: U.S. Government Printing Office, 1970), pp. 433, 447.

27. U.S. Commission on Civil Rights, *Education*, Book 2 (Washington, D.C.: U.S. Government Printing Office, 1961), p. 13.

28. Gary Orfield, *The Reconstruction of Southern Education* (N.Y.: Wiley Interscience, 1969), pp. 262, 302.

29. U.S. Commission on Civil Rights, "Federal Enforcement of School Desegregation," September 11, 1969, p. 7.

30. U.S. Commission on Civil Rights, *Political Participation* (Washington, D.C.: U.S. Government Printing Office, 1968), pp. 11-12, 189, 202-211.

31. U.S. Commission on Civil Rights, *Civil Rights Digest* (Washington, D.C.: U.S. Government Printing Office, August 1964).

32. Charles C. Moskos, Jr., "Racial Integration in the Armed Forces," in *Blacks in the United States*, edited by Norval D. Glenn and Charles M. Bonjean (San Francisco: Chandler Publishing Co., 1969), pp. 555-558.

33. U.S. Department of Labor, Bureau of Labor Statistics, *The Negroes in the United States: Their Economic and Social Situation*, Bulletin No. 1511, 1966, Table III A-1, p. 138. U.S. Department of Commerce, "Selected Characteristics of Persons and Families," *Population Characteristics*, Bureau of Census Series P-20, No. 189, August 18, 1969, p. 4.

34. Broom and Glenn, *Occupations*, p. 25.

35. Dale L. Hiestand, *Economic Growth and Employment Opportunities for Minorities* (N.Y.: Columbia University Press, 1964), p. 42.

36. Samuel Krislov, "Government and Equal Employment Opportunity," in *Employment, Race, and Poverty*, edited by Arthur M. Ross and Herbert Hill (N.Y.: Harcourt, Brace and World, Inc., 1967), pp. 348-9.

37. Chuck Stone, *Black Political Power in America* (N.Y.: Bobbs-Merrill Co., 1968), pp. 69-72.

38. Cited in *Time*, April 6, 1970, p. 94.

39. Harold M. Baron, et al, "Black Powerlessness in Chicago," *Trans-Action*, 1968.

40. Norval D. Glenn, "Changes in Social and Economic Conditions of Black Americans during the 1960's" in *Blacks in the United States*, edited by Norval D. Glenn and Charles M. Bonjean (San Francisco: Chandler Publishing Co., 1969), p. 46.

41. Moskos, *Integration*, pp. 557-559.

42. Ibid., pp. 560-561.

43. Ibid., p. 561.

44. U.S. Commission on Civil Rights, *Civil Rights 1963* (Washington, D.C.: U.S. Government Printing Office, 1963), p. 179.

45. Ibid.

46. Ray Marshall, *The Negro Worker* (N.Y.: Random House, 1967), p. 90.

47. John E. Hutchinson, "The AFL-CIO and the Negro" in *Employment, Race, and Poverty*, edited by Arthur M. Ross and Herbert Hill (N.Y.: Harcourt, Brace and World, 1967), p. 416.

48. Marshall, *Negro Worker*, p. 63.

49. Herbert Hill, "The Racial Practices of Organized Labor," in *The Negro and the American Labor Movement*, edited by Julius Jacobson (Doubleday, Garden City, N.Y., 1968), p. 292.

50. Ibid., pp. 296-297.

51. Ibid., p. 297.

52. U.S. Commission on Civil Rights, *Civil Rights 1963* (Washington, D.C.: U.S. Government Printing Office, 1963), pp. 119-122.

53. Stone, *Political Power*, p. 155.

54. Orfield, *Reconstruction*, p. 20.

55. U.S. Commission on Civil Rights, "Federal Enforcement of School Desegregation," September 11, 1969, p. 31.

56. Ibid., p. 8.

57. U.S. Commission on Civil Rights, *Racial Isolation in the Public Schools* (Washington, D.C.: U.S. Government Printing Office, 1967), p. 8.

58. *Report of the National Advisory Commission on Civil Disorders* (N.Y.: Bantam Books, 1968), pp. 426-427.

59. Glenn, *Changes*, p. 49.

60. Ibid., p. 50.

61. Cited in *Time*, July 13, 1970, p. 32.

62. Cited in the *Rocky Mountain News*, Denver, Colorado, Nov. 27, 1970, byline by William Steif, p. 102.

63. *Time*, July 13, 1970, p. 32.

64. Ibid.

65. *Report of the National Advisory Commission on Civil Disorders* (N.Y.: Bantam Books, 1968), pp. 246-247, and Karl and Alma Taeuber, *Negroes in Cities* (Chicago: Aldine Publishing Co., 1965).

66. Ibid., p. 243.

67. Jack Rosenthal, by-line in the *Denver Post*, July 12, 1970, pp. 1, 7.

68. John H. Denton, *Apartheid American Style* (Berkeley, California: Diablo Press, 1967), p. 43.

69. McEntire, *Residence and Race*, pp. 287-290.

70. Ibid.

71. Denton, *Apartheid*, pp. 50-51.

72. Ibid., p. 37.

73. Ibid.

74. Rose Helper, *Racial Policies and Practices of Real Estate Brokers* (Minneapolis: University of Minnesota Press, 1969), pp. 42, 46; Lee, p. 44.

75. Denton, *Apartheid*, p. 48.

76. Helper, *Racial Policies*, pp. 42-46.

77. Karl E. Taueber, "Residential Segregation," *Scientific American*, August 1965, p. 9; and cited in Denton, p. 43.

78. Stone, *Political Power*, pp. 228-229.

79. Voting Education Project of the Southern Regional Council.

80. United States Commission on Civil Rights, *Political Participation* (Washington, D.C.: U.S. Government Printing Office, 1968), pp. 171-174.

81. Stone, *Political Power*, p. 40.

82. *Time*, April 6, 1970, p. 27.

83. Stone, *Political Power*, pp. 76-77.

84. Norval D. Glenn, "Changes in the Social and Economic Conditions of Black Americans during the 1960's," in *Blacks in the United States*, edited by Norval D. Glenn and Charles M. Bonjean (San Francisco: Chandler Publishing Co., 1969), p. 44.

Chapter 4
**Major Independent Variables Affecting
Policy Effectiveness**

1. James L. Price, *Organizational Effectiveness* (Homewood, Illinois: Richard D. Irwin, Inc., 1968), pp. 2-3.

2. *The Denver Post*, November 22, 1970, p. 1, byline by John Herbers.

3. Gary Orfield, *The Reconstruction of Southern Education* (New York: Wiley-Interscience, 1969), p. 88.

4. Ibid., pp. 85-94.

5. Ibid., p. 90.

6. Ibid., pp. 178-180.

7. Ibid., pp. 151-207.

8. "Statement of Howard A. Glickstein, Staff Director-Designate, U.S. Commission on Civil Rights, Before the Senate Subcommittee on Labor of the Committee on Labor and Public Welfare," U.S. Civil Rights Commission, September 10, 1969, pp. 20-21.

9. U.S. Commission on Civil Rights, *Federal Civil Rights Enforcement Effort* (Washington, D.C.: U.S. Government Printing Office, 1970), pp. 220-221.

10. Glickstein, *Statement*, p. 22.

11. *Federal Civil Rights Enforcement Effort*, p. 272.

12. Ibid., p. 282.

13. Ibid., pp. 291, 308, 319.

14. Ibid., p. 283.

15. U.S. Commission on Civil Rights, "Federal Enforcement of School Segregation," September 11, 1969, pp. 47-48.

16. U.S. Commission on Civil Rights, *Political Participation* (Washington, D.C.: U.S. Government Printing Office, 1968), p. 169.

17. *Federal Civil Rights Enforcement Effort*, p. 242.

18. Ibid., pp. 345-346.

19. Ibid., pp. 1037-1038.

20. Orfield, *Reconstruction*, pp. 104-105.

21. Price, *Organizational*, p. 96.

22. Ibid.

23. Ibid., p. 98.

24. Daniel P. Moynihan, *Maximum Feasible Misunderstanding* (New York: Free Press, 1969), p. 191.

25. Glickstein, *Statement*, pp. 24-26.

26. *Employment, 1961, Book III*, U.S. Civil Rights Commission (Washington, D.C.: U.S. Government Printing Office, 1961), p. 3.

27. "Evaluation of Title VI of Civil Rights Act of 1964, U.S. Department of Agriculture," U.S. Commission on Civil Rights 20425, July 1968, p. 46.

28. Orfield, *Reconstruction*, p. 248.

29. Paul N. Norgren, "Fair Employment Practice Laws—Experience, Effects, Prospects," in *Employment, Race, and Poverty*, edited by Arthur M. Ross and Herbert Hill (New York: Harcourt, Brace and World, 1967), pp. 546-552; P.H. Norgren and S.E. Hill, *Toward Fair Employment* (New York: Columbia University Press, 1964), Chapter 7.

30. Gilbert and Eaton, *Favoritism*, pp. 45-58.

31. John Dewey, *Intelligence in the Modern World*, (New York: Modern Library, Random House, 1939), p. 951.

32. Ibid., p. 952.

33. *Federal Civil Rights Enforcement Effort*, pp. 488-489.

34. Ibid., p. 448.

35. Ibid., p. 452.

36. Ibid., p. 1053.

37. Ibid., pp. 493-495.

38. Eley and Casstevens, p. 15.

39. *Federal Civil Rights Enforcement Effort*, p. 342, (a statement by Chairman Brown of EEOC in April 1969).

40. Ibid., p. 333.

41. Ibid., p. 418.

42. Ibid., p. 164.

43. Ibid., p. 258.

44. Ibid., p. 252.

45. Glickstein, *Statement*, p. 30.

46. U.S. Commission on Civil Rights, "Federal Enforcement of School Desegregation," September 11, 1969, Appendix B.

47. *The Denver Post*, October 20, 1970, p. 8.

48. *The Rocky Mountain News* (Associated Press), December 18, 1970, p. 31.

49. U.S. Commission on Civil Rights, *Political Participation* (Washington, D.C.: U.S. Government Printing Office, 1968), p. 155.

50. Jack Greenberg, *Race Relations and American Law* (New York: Columbia University Press, 1959), pp. 15-16.

51. Denton, *Apartheid*, pp. 11-12.

52. Orfield, *Reconstruction*, p. 18.

53. Glickstein, *Statement*, p. 9.

54. Norgren, *Fair Employment*, p. 552.

55. Michael Sovern, *Legal Restraints on Racial Discrimination in Employment* (New York: Twentieth Century Fund, 1966), pp. 206-7, and Norgren, *Fair Employment*, pp. 557-563, and Greenberg, *Race Relations*, pp. 16-17.

56. Norval D. Glenn, "The Role of White Resistance and Facilitation in the Negro Struggle for Equality," in *Power and the Black Community*, edited by Sethard Fisher (New York: Random House, 1970), p. 414. This article appeared originally in *Phylon*, Summer, 1965, Volume 26, pp. 105-116.

57. Norval D. Glenn, "White Gains from Negro Subordination," *Blacks in the United States*, edited by Norval D. Glenn and Charles M. Bonjean (San Francisco: Chandler Publishing Co., 1969), p. 289. This article first appeared in *Social Problems*, 14 (Fall, 1966), pp. 159-178.

58. Howard S. Becker and Irving Louis Horowitz, "The Culture of Civility," *Trans-Action*, April 1970, Vol. 7, No. 6.

59. George Eaton Simpson and J. Milton Yinger, *Racial and Cultural Minorities* (New York: Harper and Row, 1965), p. 536.

60. Norval D. Glenn, "The Role of White Resistance and Facilitation in the Negro Struggle for Equality," in *Power and the Black Community*, edited by Sethard Fisher (New York: Random House, 1970), p. 420.

61. Pinkney, *Black Americans*, pp. 202-203.

62. Robert O. Blood, Jr., *Northern Breakthrough* (Belmont, California: Wadsworth Publishing Co., Inc., 1968), pp. 90-96.

63. August Meier, "Civil Rights Strategies for Negro Employment," in *Employment, Race, and Poverty*, edited by Arthur M. Ross and Herbert Hill (New York: Harcourt, Brace and World, 1967), p. 193.

64. Ibid., p. 194.

65. Marshall, *Negro Worker*, p. 152.

66. Norgren, *Fair Employment*, p. 555.

67. Meier, *Civil*, pp. 197-8.

68. Ibid., p. 195.

69. Orfield, *Reconstruction*, pp. 24-5.

70. Robert A. Thompson, Hylan Lewis, and Davis McEntire, "Atlanta and Birmingham, A Comparative Study in Negro Housing," in *Studies in Housing and Minority Groups*, edited by Nathan Glazer and Davis McEntire (Berkeley: University of California Press, 1960), p. 83.

71. *Political Participation*, U.S. Commission on Civil Rights (Washington, D.C.: U.S. Government Printing Office, 1968), p. 155.

72. Orfield, *Reconstruction*, pp. 267-8.

73. *The Denver Post*, September 7, 1970, p. 14.

74. Donald R. Matthews, "Political Science Research on Race Relations," in *Race and the Social Sciences*, edited by Irwin Katz and Patricia Gurin (New York: Basic Books, 1969), pp. 117-132.

75. Robert Blake and Wayne Dennis, "The Development of Stereotypes Concerning the Negro," *Journal of Abnormal and Social Psychology*, 38, 1943, 525-31. Mary E. Goodman, *Race Awareness in Young Children* (Cambridge: Addison-Wesley, 1952). Kenneth J. Moreland, "Racial Recognition by Nursery School Children in Lynchburg, Virginia," *Social Forces*, 37, 1958, 132-7. Eugene L. Horowitz and Ruth E. Horowitz, "Development of Social Attitudes in Children," *Sociometry*, 1, 1938, 301-38. Olive W. Quinn, "The Transmission of Racial Attitudes Among Southerners," *Social Forces*, 33, 1954, 41-47. William McCord, Joan McCord and Alan Howard, "Early Familial Experiences and Bigotry," *American Sociological Review*, 25, 1960, pp. 717-722.

76. Milton L. Barron, "A Content Analysis of Intergroup Humor," *American Sociological Review*, 15, 1950, 88-94. Robert J. Hamblin, "The Dynamics of Racial Discrimination," *Social Problems*, 10, 1962, 103-120. Leonard I. Pearlin, "Shifting Group Attachments and Attitudes Toward Negroes," *Social Forces*, 33, 1954, 47-50. Muzafer Sherif, "Experiments in Group Conflict," *Scientific American*, 195, 1956, 54-8.

77. Michael J. Ross, Thomas Crawford, and Thomas Pettigrew, "Negro-Neighbors-Banned in Boston," *Trans-Action*, 3, No. 6, 1966, 13-18. Robin Williams, *Strangers Next Door* (Englewood Cliffs, New Jersey: Prentice-Hall, 1964). Bruno Bettelheim and Morris Janowitz, *Dynamics of Prejudice: A Psychological and Sociological Study of Veterans* (New York: Harper and Row, 1950). Nathan Ackerman and Marie Jahoda, *Anti-Semitism and Emotional Disorder* (New York: Harper and Row, 1950). Frank R. Westie and David H. Howard, "Social Status Differentials and the Race Attitudes of Negroes," *American Sociological Review*, 19, 1954, 584-591. Seymour Feshbach and

Robert Singer, "The Effects of Personal and Shared Threats Upon Social Prejudice," *Journal of Abnormal and Social Psychology*, 54, 1957, 411-416.

78. Milton Rokeach, *The Open and Closed Mind* (New York: Basic Books, Inc., 1960). C.E. Izard, "Personality Similarity and Friendship," *American Psychologist*, 14, 1959. A.J. Lott and J. Rosell, "Race, Sex, and Assumed Similarity," *American Psychologist*, 14, 1959. H. Rosenfeld and J. Jackson, "Effect of Similarity of Personalities on Interpersonal Attraction," *American Psychologist*, 14, 1959, 366-367. Donn Byrne and Terry Wong, "Interpersonal Attraction and Assumed Dissimilarity of Attitudes," *Journal of Abnormal and Social Psychology*, October 1962, 246-253.

79. Harold L. Sheppard, "The Negro-Merchant: A Study of Negro Anti-Semitism," *American Journal of Sociology*, 53, 1957, pp. 96-99. Daniel Glaser, "The Sentiments of Soldiers Abroad Toward Europeans," *American Journal of Sociology*, 51, 1946, 433-438. Judith T. Shuval, "Emerging Patterns of Ethnic Strain in Israel," *Social Forces*, 40, 1962, 323-330. Muzafer Sherif, "Experiments in Group Conflict," *Scientific American*, 195, 1956, 54-8.

80. T.W. Adorno, et al, *The Authoritarian Personality* (New York: Harper and Row, 1950). A.H. Roberts and Milton Rokeach, "Anomie, Authoritarianism and Prejudice: A Replication," *American Journal of Sociology*, January 1956, 355-8.

81. Arnold Rose, *The Roots of Prejudice* (UNESCO, 1961), p. 8. James W. Parkes, *An Enemy of the People: Anti-Semitism* (Penguin, 1946).

82. McEntire, *Residence and Race*, p. 355.

83. Vander Zanden, *Race Relations in Transition: The Segregation Crisis Within the South* (New York: Random House, Inc., 1965), p. 54.

84. Lewis M. Killian, *White Southerners* (New York: Random House, 1970), pp. 66-7.

85. Raymond J. Murphy and Howard Elinson, *Problems and Prospects of the Negro Movement* (Belmont, California: Wadsworth Publishing Co., 1968), p. 14.

86. William Brink and Louis Harris, "What Whites Think of Negroes," in *Problems and Prospects of the Negro Movement* (Belmont, California: Wadsworth Publishing Co., 1968), p. 26.

87. Ibid., p. 26.

88. Frank R. Westie, "The American Dilemma: An Empirical Test," in *Blacks in the United States*, edited by Norval D. Glenn and Charles M. Bonjean, pp. 206-7. Reprinted from the *American Sociological Review*, 30 (August 1965), 527-538.

89. A. Campbell and H. Schuman, "White Beliefs about Negroes," in *Black Americans and White Racism*, edited by Marcel L. Goldschmid (New York: Holt, Rinehart and Winston, 1970), p. 272. Reprinted from *Racial Attitudes in Fifteen American Cities*, Supplemental Studies for the National Advisory

Commission on Civil Disorders (Washington, D.C.: U.S. Government Printing Office, 1968), pp. 29-38.

90. Brink and Harris, *What Whites Think*, p. 27.

91. Cited in Gilbert and Eaton, *Favoritism*, p. 40.

92. Eley and Casstevens, *Fair-Housing*, p. 17.

93. Ibid., p. 8.

94. Orfield, *Reconstruction*, p. 32.

95. Ibid., p. 33.

96. Ibid., p. 34.

97. Ibid., p. 294.

98. Ibid., p. 284.

99. Gilbert and Eaton, *Favoritism*, p. 40.

100. *Newsweek*, February 15, 1965.

101. A. Campbell and H. Schuman, "Black Views of Racial Issues," in *Black Americans and White Racism* (New York: Holt, Rinehart, and Winston, 1970), edited by Marcel L. Goldschmid, pp. 346-365.

102. Cited in Killian, *White*, p. 136.

103. Albert Pepitone and W. Wallace, "Experimental Studies on the Dynamics of Hostility." Paper read at Pennsylvania Psychological Association Meetings, 1955. Described in Albert Pepitone, "Attributions of Causality, Social Attitudes, and Cognitive Matching Processes," in *Person Perception and Interpersonal Behavior*, edited by Renato Tagiuri and Luigi Petrullo (Stanford: Stanford University Press, 1958).

104. Martin T. Orne and Frederick J. Evans, "Social Control in the Psychological Experiment," *Journal of Personality and Social Psychology*, 1, 1965, 189-200. Cited in William Gamson, *Power and Discontent* (Homewood, Illinois: Dorsey Press, 1968), p. 130.

105. Cited in Gamson, *Power*, pp. 132-3.

106. Ibid., p. 134.

107. Ibid.

108. Vander Zanden, *Race Relations in Transition: The Segregation Crisis Within the South* (New York: Random House, Inc., 1965), p. 74.

109. Norgren, *Fair Employment*, p. 566.

110. Herbert R. Northrup, "Industry's Racial Employment Policies," in *Employment, Race, and Poverty* (New York: Harcourt, Brace and World, 1967), edited by Arthur M. Ross and Herbert Hill, p. 304.

111. John P. Dean and Alex Rosen, *A Manual of Intergroup Relations* (Chicago: University of Chicago Press, 1955).

112. Blood, *Breakthrough*, pp. 47-8.

113. Orfield, *Reconstruction*, pp. 17-18.

114. Ibid., pp. 303-4.

115. Ibid., p. 287.

116. Greenberg, *American Law*, p. 25.

117. Marshall, *Negro Worker*, p. 146.

118. S.M. Miller and Frank Riessman, *Social Class and Social Policy* (New York: Basic Books, 1968), pp. 7-23; 121-2; 144; 153; 198-199; 207-8.

119. Leonard Broom and Norval D. Glenn, "When Will America's Negroes Catch Up?" in *Power and the Black Community*, edited by Sethard Fisher (N.Y.: Random House, 1970), p. 410.

About the Author

Richard M. Burkey is Assistant Professor of Sociology and a member of the Center of International Race Relations, University of Denver. A native of Colorado, he completed his undergraduate studies at the University of Denver and earned his MA and PhD from the University of Colorado. His major areas of interest are race relations and social stratification. He is currently at work on a sociology textbook with Wilbert C. Moore. In addition, he is engaged in a National Science Foundation study on pollution and policy sponsored through the Denver Research Institute.